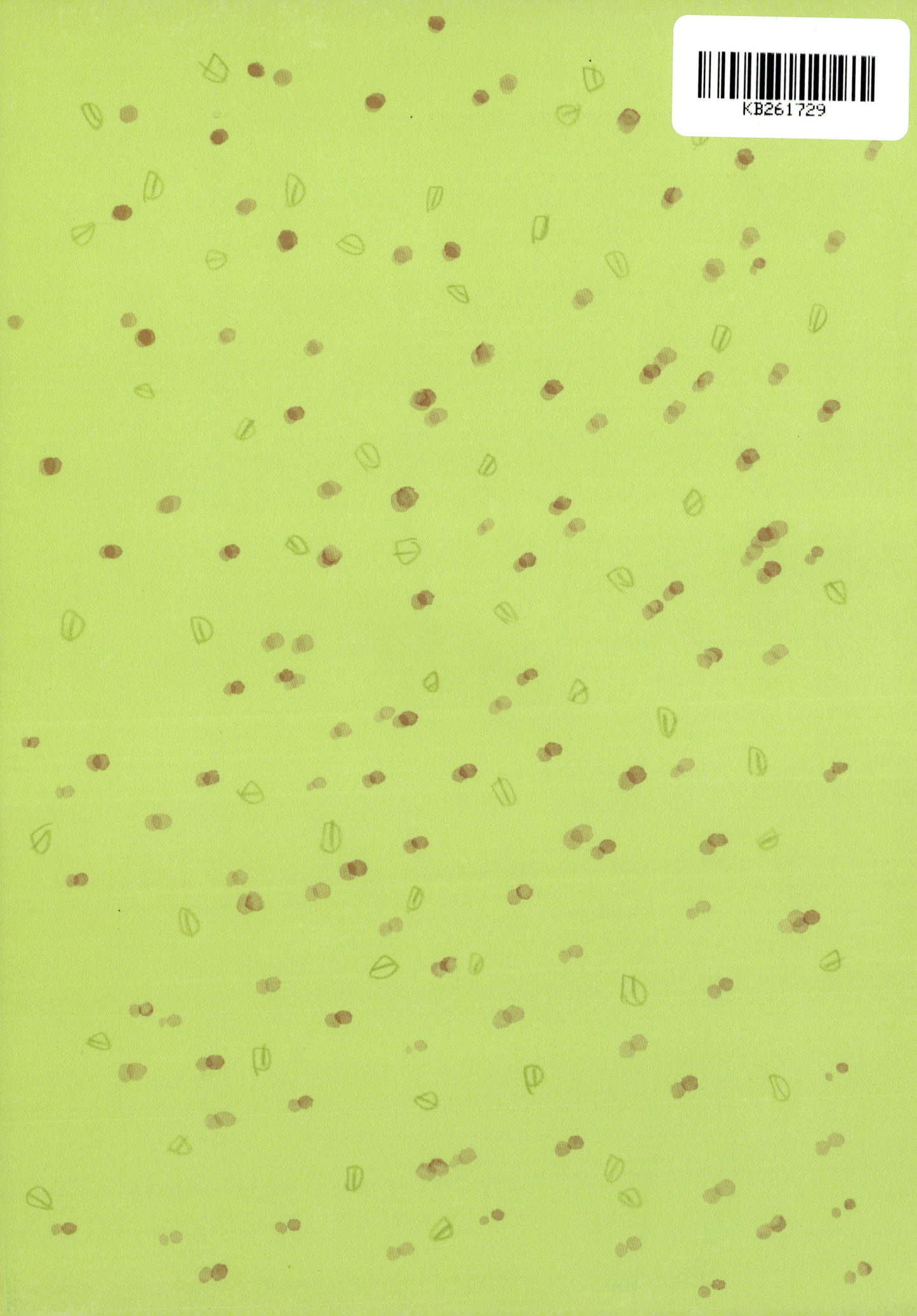

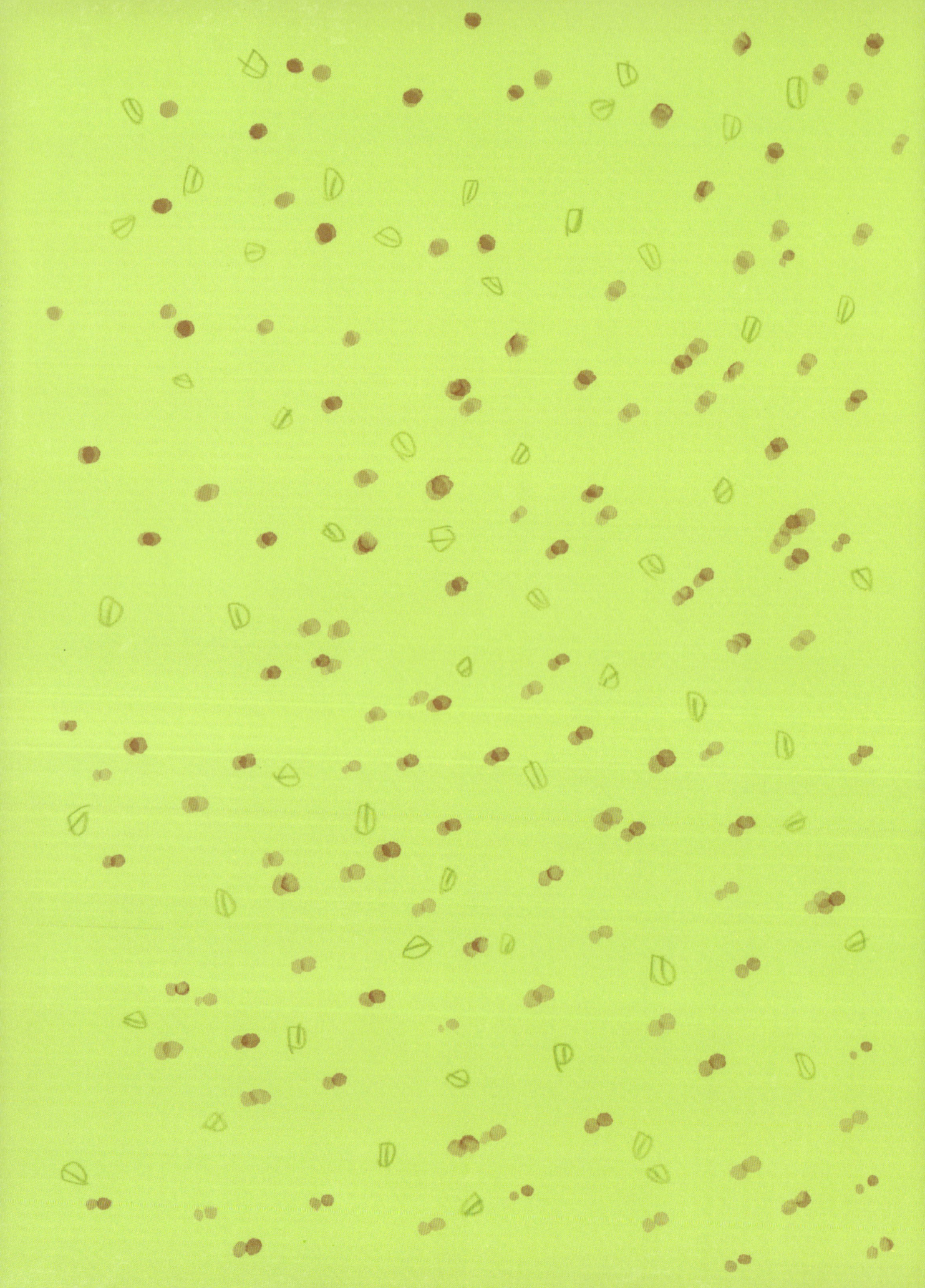

complete **Reading Fundamentals**

Reading
Leader

L301

Intermediate

Steve Gary Brown ELT Research Center

saramin

Preface

Nobody doubts that reading is one of the most essential tools for obtaining information. People have been reading since the beginning of human history. Good reading skills allow one to interpret ideas more effectively, making reading an important key to success. As the world gets smaller and more connected, finding all the information that we need translated into our native language can be difficult. Therefore, learning foreign languages is becoming increasingly important. English is the most popular language in the world, which is why we need to learn English and learn to read it well. However, reading well is not easy as we'd like it to be. Sometimes we run into unfamiliar cultural references, or encounter unknown words. We may not even be aware of how much of the reading material we truly understand. Reading Leader is designed to help students who are in an EFL (English as a foreign language) environment start reading properly and improve their reading capability as they progress through each level.

The features of Reading Leader are detailed below:

1. A wide variety of topics that are closely related to school curriculum not only help students avoid feeling frustrated by unfamiliar cultural references, but also help build up the confidence to deal with a diversity of subjects.

2. Each book contains word lists of 200-250 words to help you build up your vocabulary skills. That means you'll study 600-750 words for each level, and almost 3000 on completion of the series.

3. You can assess your reading and writing ability through Comprehension Check-Up and Sum Up. Also, since those questions are developed to meet the standards for NEAT (National English Ability Test), students can use this book to competently prepare for NEAT.

We hope that this book and your English knowledge will help you to achieve your future goals.

Steve Gary Brown ELT Research Center

Table of **Contents**

Syllabus

Topic	Title	Word Count	Type	Level of Difficulty	Reading Strategies
UNIT 01 Language & Literature	Taking from the Rich and Giving to the Poor	263	Advertisement	★★★★	Finding the main idea or topic
UNIT 02 Mathematics	Feeling Negative	290	Diary	★★	Identifying the author's purpose
UNIT 03 Mathematics	Not Exactly, but Close Enough	288	Expository essay	★★	Understanding attitude
UNIT 04 Science	Your Most Important Muscle	262	Conversation	★★	Making inferences
UNIT 05 Science	60,000 Miles of Tubes	293	Lecture	★★★	Intensive reading
UNIT 06 Science	Atoms	251	Letter	★★★★	Extensive reading
UNIT 07 Science	What's inside an Atom?	254	Conversation	★★★★★	Scanning
UNIT 08 Science	How the Wind Blows	250	Lecture	★★★	Skimming
UNIT 09 Geoscience	Let's Be Cartographers!	293	Presentation	★★★★	Identifying time order
UNIT 10 Geoscience	So Different!	283	Letter	★	Understanding the details
UNIT 11 History	After the Roman Empire	288	Letter	★★★	Guessing unknown words in context
UNIT 12 History	Not So Dark After All	279	Expository essay	★★★★	Making inferences
UNIT 13 Architecture	Famous Buildings in Europe	278	Letter	★★	Previewing and making predictions
UNIT 14 Arts	The Little Wizard	224	Expository essay	★	Paraphrasing
UNIT 15 Arts	The Fifth Symphony	247	Lecture	★★★	Drawing conclusions
UNIT 16 Health & Life	What Type of Exercise Should I Do?	255	Letter	★★	Summarizing

How to Use This **Book**

Step 1. **Read** and Comprehension **Check-Up**

Each book has 16 Units featuring a wide variety of subjects related to school curriculum. This will ==help you to acquire cultural knowledge and build up the confidence to deal with all types of subjects.== You can also assess your understanding of the reading materials with ==well-developed questions that are compatible with NEAT.==

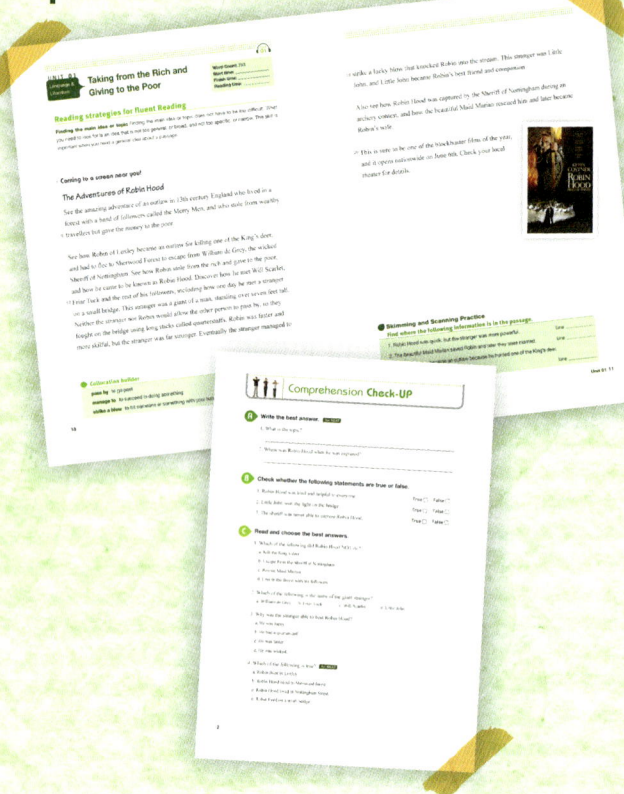

Step 2. Vocabulary **Power-UP**

Check the progress of your vocabulary knowledge by matching words in context, understanding the relationship between words, and identifying synonyms using context clues. ==Improve your ability to guess the meaning of unknown words without relying on a dictionary.==

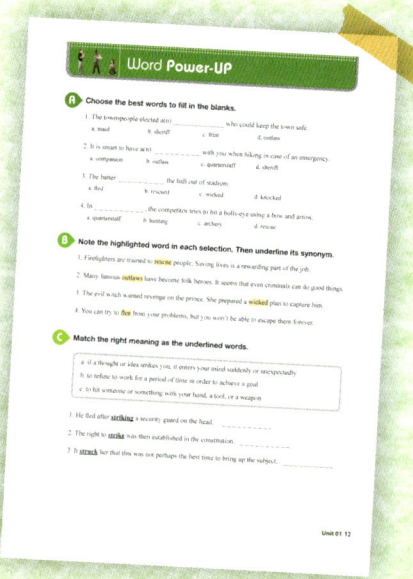

Step 3. Sum UP!

This section gives the reader an insight into how to summarize a passage after reading. This section also provides a variety of writing activities making it helpful when preparing for a writing test or when writing for oneself.

※ All the MP3 files and supplementary materials containing answer keys, Korean translations, and word lists are available for download at www.saramin.com

UNIT 01 Taking from the Rich and Giving to the Poor

Subject: Language & Literature
Type: Advertisement
Word Count: 263
Level of Difficulty: ★ ★ ★ ★

Before You Read

• **Think about the following questions.**

1. What is Robin Hood famous for?
2. Who is one of your heroes?

Word Preview

• **Match the words to the correct definitions.**

1. _____ evil in actions or ideas

2. _____ a person who often breaks the law; criminal

3. _____ to catch someone so that they become your prisoner

4. _____ to save someone from a dangerous or unpleasant situation

5. _____ someone who is with you

6. _____ to hit someone or something and force it somewhere

7. _____ to run away; escape

8.
_____

9.
_____

10.
_____

outlaw	flee	wicked	sheriff	friar	knock
companion	capture	archery	rescue		

UNIT 01
Language & Literature

Taking from the Rich and Giving to the Poor

Word Count: 263
Start time: _____
Finish time: _____
Reading time: _____

Reading strategies for fluent Reading

Finding the main idea or topic Finding the main idea or topic does not have to be too difficult. What you need to look for is an idea that is not too general, or broad, and not too specific, or narrow. This skill is important when you need a general idea about a passage.

1 **Coming to a screen near you!**

The Adventures of Robin Hood

See the amazing adventure of an outlaw in 13th century England who lived in a forest with a band of followers called the Merry Men, and who stole from wealthy
5 travellers but gave the money to the poor.

See how Robin of Loxley became an outlaw for killing one of the King's deer, and had to flee to Sherwood Forest to escape from William de Grey, the wicked Sheriff of Nottingham. See how Robin stole from the rich and gave to the poor, and how he came to be known as Robin Hood. Discover how he met Will Scarlet,
10 Friar Tuck and the rest of his followers, including how one day he met a stranger on a small bridge. This stranger was a giant of a man, standing over seven feet tall. Neither the stranger nor Robin would allow the other person to pass by, so they fought on the bridge using long sticks called quarterstaffs. Robin was faster and more skilful, but the stranger was far stronger. Eventually the stranger managed to

● **Collocation builder**

pass by to go past

manage to to succeed in doing something

strike a blow to hit someone or something with your hand

15 strike a lucky blow that knocked Robin into the stream. This stranger was Little John, and Little John became Robin's best friend and companion.

Also see how Robin Hood was captured by the Sheriff of Nottingham during an archery contest, and how the beautiful Maid Marian rescued him and later became Robin's wife.

20 This is sure to be one of the blockbuster films of the year, and it opens nationwide on June 6th. Check your local theater for details.

🍃 Skimming and Scanning Practice
Find where the following information is in the passage.

1. Robin Hood was quick, but the stranger was more powerful.	Line _____
2. The beautiful Maid Marian saved Robin and later they were married.	Line _____
3. Robin of Loxley became an outlaw because he hunted one of the King's deer.	
	Line _____

Comprehension Check-UP

A ▸ **Write the best answer.** for NEAT

1. What is the topic?

_____

2. Where was Robin Hood when he was captured?

_____

B ▸ **Check whether the following statements are true or false.**

1. Robin Hood was kind and helpful to everyone.   True ☐ False ☐

2. Little John won the fight on the bridge.   True ☐ False ☐

3. The sheriff was never able to capture Robin Hood.   True ☐ False ☐

C ▸ **Read and choose the best answers.**

1. Which of the following did Robin Hood NOT do?
   a. Kill the King's deer
   b. Escape from the Sheriff of Nottingham
   c. Rescue Maid Marian
   d. Live in the forest with his followers

2. Which of the following is the name of the giant stranger?
   a. William de Grey   b. Friar Tuck   c. Will Scarlet   d. Little John

3. Why was the stranger able to beat Robin Hood?
   a. He was lucky.
   b. He had a quarterstaff.
   c. He was faster.
   d. He was wicked.

4. Which of the following is true? for NEAT
   a. Robin lived in Loxley.
   b. Robin Hood lived in Sherwood forest.
   c. Robin Hood lived in Nottingham forest.
   d. Robin lived on a small bridge.

Word Power-UP

A ▶ Choose the best words to fill in the blanks.

1. The townspeople elected a(n) _____ who could keep the town safe.

   a. maid   b. sheriff   c. friar   d. outlaw

2. It is smart to have a(n) _____ with you when hiking in case of an emergency.

   a. companion   b. outlaw   c. quarterstaff   d. sheriff

3. The batter _____ the ball out of stadium.

   a. fled   b. rescued   c. wicked   d. knocked

4. In _____, the competitor tries to hit a bulls-eye using a bow and arrow.

   a. quarterstaff   b. hunting   c. archery   d. rescue

B ▶ Note the highlighted word in each selection. Then underline its synonym.

1. Firefighters are trained to rescue people. Saving lives is a rewarding part of the job,

2. Many famous outlaws have become folk heroes. It seems that even criminals can do good things.

3. The evil witch wanted revenge on the prince. She prepared a wicked plan to capture him.

4. You can try to flee from your problems, but you won't be able to escape them forever.

C ▶ Match the right meaning as the underlined words.

> a. if a thought or idea strikes you, it enters your mind suddenly or unexpectedly
>
> b. to refuse to work for a period of time in order to achieve a goal
>
> c. to hit someone or something with your hand, a tool, or a weapon

1. He fled after **striking** a security guard on the head. _____

2. The right to **strike** was then established in the constitution. _____

3. It **struck** her that this was not perhaps the best time to bring up the subject. _____

Step 1. Sentence Completion

Draw a line between A and B to complete each sentence.

A

1. In the forest, he would rob from the rich

2. Eventually, the Sheriff captured him

3. Maid Marian rescued Robin Hood

4. Robin of Loxley became an outlaw

5. He fled from the Sheriff of Nottingham

B

a. after killing the King's deer.

b. and they got married.

c. during an archery contest.

d. into Sherwood forest.

e. and give to the poor.

Step 2. Sequencing

Put the sentences in the correct order.

The Story of Robin Hood

1. _____

2. _____

3. _____

4. _____

5. _____

Subject: Mathematics
Type: Diary
Word Count: 290
Level of Difficulty: ★ ★

Before You Read

• **Think about the following questions.**

1. What is a number scale?
2. Which is the larger number, -4 or -6?

Word Preview

• **Match the words to the correct definitions.**

1. _____ to a smaller degree or amount

2. _____ believing that good things will happen; higher than zero (↔ negative)

3. _____ a longer distance; more

4. _____ in a way that is clear for almost anyone; clearly

5. _____ the process of finding the total of two or more numbers (↔ subtraction)

6. _____ an amount of money

addition	obviously	sum	positive	further	less

Feeling Negative

Word Count: 290
Start time: _____
Finish time: _____
Reading time: _____

Reading strategies for fluent Reading

Identifying the author's purpose Some questions will ask you to identify an author's purpose. This usually means figuring out why the author talks about something or someone or why the author uses a particular word or phrase. In order to do this, you need to figure out how the phrase or specific topic is related to the ideas around it.

1 Dear Diary,

I'm feeling very negative at the moment. But don't worry. It is just that I now understand negative numbers! If a number is less than 0, it is a negative number, and negative numbers have a minus sign in front of them, like this: '-4.' Negative

5 numbers are sort of the other way round from positive numbers. In positive numbers 5 is obviously bigger than 4, but in negative numbers -4 is bigger than -5. This makes sense if you think about a number scale:

$$-5 \ -4 \ -3 \ -2 \ -1 \ \ 0 \ \ 1 \ \ 2 \ \ 3 \ \ 4 \ \ 5$$

The further to the right of the scale you go, the bigger the number is. As you can
10 see, -4 is further to the right of the scale than -5. Actually, I knew that already, but today I finally worked out how to do addition and subtraction with negative numbers, so I'm actually feeling very positive about myself!!!

● Collocation builder

sort of kind or type of

the other way round in the opposite order or position

make sense to be a good reason or explanation for something

work out to solve a problem by doing a calculation

Here's how you do it.

If you are subtracting two negative numbers, you actually add the numbers
15 together! So -7 minus -3 is written as -7 - -3. Subtracting a negative from a
negative means the sum becomes less negative. In other words, you add a positive
to a negative number. So -7 + 3 equals -4. Again, just think of the number scale,
because we are adding numbers together it gets bigger, and therefore it goes to the
right on the scale.
20 Adding minus numbers makes them more negative. That becomes a subtraction.
So -7 plus -3 is -10. It was very confusing at first, but after a bit of practice using
the number scale I now understand negative numbers completely.

I'm going to sleep now. I'll write in you again
tomorrow! Good night, Diary.

Skimming and Scanning Practice
Find where the following information is in the passage.

1. The more to the right of the scale, the larger the number is.	Line _____
2. When subtracting negative numbers, you really add them.	Line _____
3. Numbers below 0 are negative numbers.	Line _____

A Write the best answer. `for NEAT`

1. What is the topic?

_____

2. What does the author recommend using to understand negative numbers?

_____

B Check whether the following statements are true or false.

1. Numbers below zero are negative.   True ☐   False ☐

2. Negative 6 is bigger than negative 3.   True ☐   False ☐

3. The author finds the number scale useful.   True ☐   False ☐

C Read and choose the best answers.

1. Which of the following is NOT true about the number scale?

   a. The further to left the larger the number.

   b. Positive numbers are on the right side.

   c. It is helpful for understanding negative numbers.

   d. Negative numbers are on the left side.

2. Which of the following made the author feel positive?

   a. Getting a good score on her test

   b. Writing a diary entry about negative numbers

   c. Knowing how to add and subtract negative numbers

   d. She became confused by negative numbers.

3. Which of the following is true?   `for NEAT`

   a. Adding two negative numbers becomes a subtraction.

   b. -5 minus -3 equals -2.

   c. Subtracting two negatives makes a positive.

   d. The number scale cannot help with subtraction.

A Choose the best words to fill in the blanks.

1. You shouldn't need a calculator just to do a simple _____ problem.

   a. positive   b. less   c. negative   d. subtraction

2. Even thought the movie was _____ interesting than I expected, I'm still happy that I saw it.

   a. sort   b. completely   c. less   d. further

3. The _____ away from the city, the brighter the stars became.

   a. scale   b. positive   c. further   d. practice

4. The _____ of the three baby puppies brought joy to the Park family.

   a. addition   b. numbers   c. math   d. right

B Note the highlighted word in each selection. Then underline its synonym.

1. A positive attitude can be good for your health. People who are cheery are less likely to get sick.

2. Keep your receipts in order to calculate your total expenses. You may be surprised by the sum.

3. Craig isn't usually this gloomy. Something negative must have happened to him.

4. Obviously, the average child wouldn't know how to do advanced physics. This child is clearly very bright.

C Match the appropriate meaning for the underlined word.

> a. a series of marks at set distances along a line, used for measurement
>
> b. to climb; ascend; mount
>
> c. one of the thin, flat plates forming the covering of certain animals, such as fish or lizards

1. Some thermometers have **scales** for measuring both Fahrenheit and Celsius. _____

2. Despite having **scales**, snakes' skin is surprisingly smooth. _____

3. Erik Weihenmayer was the first blind person to **scale** Mount Everest. _____

Summarizing

Complete the diagram with the words from the box below.

Introduction

Negative numbers are numbers that are less than zero. They are usually written by putting a 'minus' sign in front of the number. Doing addition and subtraction using negative numbers can be a little confusing at first, but there are some _____ to make it easier to understand.

Reason 1

To avoid confusion when adding and subtracting negative numbers, it's a good idea to use the number _____. _____ a line with numbers on it, starting with _____ in the middle and increasing along the right side of the line. Likewise, negative numbers begin to the left of zero and _____ along the left side.

Reason 2

Now, when adding two negative numbers, you are going even further to the left on the number scale. Therefore, -3 plus -4 _____ -7.

Reason 3

When you subtract one negative number from another negative number, the answer is _____ negative, in other words, more positive. You end up moving towards the right of the number scale.

• imagine	• equals	• less	• continue	• scale
• zero	• methods			

UNIT 03 Not Exactly, but Close Enough

Subject: Mathematics
Type: Expository essay
Word Count: 288
Level of Difficulty: ★★

Before You Read

• **Think about the following questions.**

1. When would knowing an approximate number be more useful than the exact number?
2. What is 33 rounded to the nearest tens?

Word Preview

• **Match the words to the correct definitions.**

1. _____ a number representing an amount, especially an official number

2. _____ a mathematical quantity shown by a letter of the alphabet or sign

3. _____ close in amount or time, but not exact (↔ exact)

4. _____ [up/down] to change an exact figure to the nearest whole number

5. _____ particular; sure; having no doubt

certain	approximate	round	value	figure	exact

UNIT 03
Mathematics

Not Exactly, but Close Enough

Word Count: 288
Start time: _____
Finish time: _____
Reading time: _____

Reading strategies for fluent Reading

Understanding attitude Attitude is a reflection of how the author feels about a topic. By choosing a certain attitude, the author informs you of his or her attitude toward a topic. Careful choice of words to express certain emotions or paint certain pictures is the author's main tool for his attitude.

1 Sometimes, we do not need to know the exact number or value of something. Maybe we do not need to know that there are exactly 2125 calories in a cake, and it is OK just to know that there are about 2000 calories. Or maybe we only need to know that the cake costs about $3.00, not that it costs $2.95.

5 So, if we only need to know the approximate number or value, we can 'round' the number up or down. Let's look at the rules for 'rounding.'

When you 'round' a number, you round it *to* a certain value. For instance, you can 'round' to the nearest 10, or the nearest 100, or the nearest 1000 and so on. So first you have to decide to what you are 'rounding to.' Are you rounding to the nearest 10 10, or the nearest 100, for instance? Then, you need to know whether to 'round up' or 'round down,' and the rules are quite simple. If the number you are rounding is followed by 5,6,7,8, or 9, you round the number up. If it is followed by 1,2,3, or 4, round the number down. Let's look at some examples using the number 6528.

1) Rounding 6528 to the nearest 10 is 6530. You round *up* the number following
15 the tens figure because it is an 8.

2) Rounding 6528 to the nearest 100 is 6500. You round *down* the number
following the hundreds figure because it is a 2.

3) Rounding 6528 to the nearest 1000 is 7000. You round *up* the number following
the thousands figure because it is a 5.

20 Notice how all the numbers to the right of the place that you are rounding are
always zeros.

● **Skimming and Scanning Practice**
   Find where the following information is in the passage.

   1. It's alright just knowing that there are about 2000 calories.   Line _____

   2. First you need to figure out the number you want to round to.   Line _____

   3. If 1, 2, 3, or 4 follow a number, you round it down.   Line _____

Comprehension Check-UP

A Write the best answer. **for NEAT**

1. What is the topic?

_____

2. How do you know when to round up?

_____

B Check whether the following statements are true or false.

1. The author feels the rules for rounding up or down are difficult.   True ☐   False ☐

2. The number right of the place you are rounding to will be zero.   True ☐   False ☐

3. Rounding is used to find an exact value.   True ☐   False ☐

C Read and choose the best answers.

1. Which of the following is determined by rounding up or down?

   a. an approximate value

   b. a hundreds figure

   c. the exact number

   d. the price of something

2. Which of the following is NOT rounded to the nearest tens?

   a. 4770   b. 8003   c. 690   d. 10

3. How do you know whether to round up or down?

   a. The figure you are rounding to determines whether you round up or down.

   b. If you are rounding to the hundreds, you must round up.

   c. You must look at the number following the place you are rounding to.

   d. If a number is between 1 and 5 you will round it down.

4. Which of the following is true? **for NEAT**

   a. A number rounded to the nearest hundred will end in zero.

   b. The rules for rounding up or down are quite difficult.

   c. 334 rounded to the nearest tens is 340.

   d. Rounding is used to find an exact value.

24

A Choose the best words to fill in the blanks.

1. The film screening will be _____ by a question and answer session with the director.
   a. subtracted   b. followed   c. added   d. rounded

2. Clark asked the lady where the _____ gas station was located.
   a. nearest   b. number   c. approximate   d. round

3. The number for pi (π), 3.141592 ..., is often _____ off to the nearest hundredth.
   a. guessed   b. exact   c. certain   d. rounded

4. Tell me the _____ time when you will be finished with your work.
   a. value   b. early   c. approximate   d. cost

B Note the highlighted word in each selection. Then underline its synonym.

1. The value of education is well known. Its worth is reflected by the many education-related businesses.

2. Accountants must be exact in their work. If the records aren't precise, big problems can occur.

3. The CEO frowned when she saw the figures. The amount of losses was more than she had expected.

4. People with diabetes can only eat certain types of foods. They have a definite reason to watch what they eat.

C Match the appropriate meaning for the underlined word.

> a. any complete course, series, or succession
>
> b. to express to the nearest ten, hundred, or thousand
>
> c. having a flat, circular surface, as a disk

1. **Rounding** up large numbers makes them easier to remember. _____

2. The nations agreed to hold another **round** of peace talks. _____

3. While most pizzas are **round**, this restaurant bakes rectangular pizzas. _____

Step 1. Rewriting

Fill in the blanks using words from the box below.

Dear Philip,

You always helped me with math so I thought I'd tell you about the newest thing I've learned. I learned about rounding numbers. It's really quite easy. We just take a(n) _____ number and turn it into a(n) _____ number. For example, the number 314 is can be rounded to 300. Just decide what _____ you want to round to, the _____ tens, hundreds, thousands, etc. Then you look at the number _____ that place and round it up or _____. If the number is from 1 to 4, you round it down. If the number is from 5 to 9, you round up. The thing I want to ask you, though, is why do we need to round numbers? How is it useful? Thanks for helping me!

Jane

• down	• approximate	• exact	• place	• nearest
• following				

Step 2. Composition

Reply to the letter as if you were Jane writing back to Philip.

UNIT 04 Your Most Important Muscle

Subject: Science
Type: Conversation
Word Count: 262
Level of Difficulty: ★★

Before You Read

• **Think about the following questions.**

1. What important function does your heart do?
2. How many chambers does a heart have?

Word Preview

• **Match the words to the correct definitions.**

1. _____ an enclosed space, especially in your body or inside a machine

2. _____ the regular movement of blood

3. _____ a gas in the air that has no smell or taste, and that all animals depend on to breathe

4. _____ to make liquid or gas move; a machine for forcing liquid or gas into or out of something

5. _____ to hit someone or something several times; if someone's heart beats, it makes the same sound and movements again and again

6.
_____

7.
_____

8.
_____

chamber	pump	oxygen	chest	fist	beat
pulse	muscle				

Your Most Important Muscle

Track
04

Word Count: 262
Start time: _____
Finish time: _____
Reading time: _____

Reading strategies for fluent Reading

Making inferences Making inferences means understanding something that is not mentioned directly. Whenever we read, we can assume certain things from the information we learn. But we must be careful not to assume too much. Everything we "infer" must be based on the information given.

1 Richard: Mum, what is the strongest muscle in my body?

Mother: Well, I'm not exactly sure, but I know which is the most important.

Richard: Hmm...is it my tongue?

Mother: No! The most important muscle in your body works every second of
5   every day, it is in your chest and is about the size of your fist. It pumps
       the blood around your body.

Richard: Oh, you mean my heart. I didn't realize it was a muscle!

Mother: Yes, it is amazing. It is actually two pumps. The right side of your heart
       gets the blood from your body and pumps it to your lungs so the blood
10   can get oxygen. And the left side of your heart gets the blood back from
       your lungs and sends it all around your body. Every time your heart
       pumps blood, we say it beats. And you know how to measure your

heartbeat, don't you?

Richard: Oh yes, I can measure my pulse. A good place to measure my pulse is on
15 the side of my neck.

Mother: Good, and every time you feel the pulse beat, that is actually your heart
pumping. By counting how many times your pulse beats in a minute,
you know your heart rate. Now, do you know the
different parts of your heart?

20 **Richard:** No!

Mother: Your heart has two sides, the right and the left.
And each of these sides is divided into a top and
a bottom, each called a chamber. So you have
four chambers in total. The chambers at the top
25 are called the atria, and the chambers at the
bottom are called the ventricles.

● Skimming and Scanning Practice
Find where the following information is in the passage.

1. The sides of your heart have tops and bottoms known as chambers.	Line _____
2. Your body's most important muscle is constantly working.	Line _____
3. When your heart pumps blood, we say that it is beating.	Line _____

A Write the best answer. **for NEAT**

1. What is the topic?

_____

2. What is a good place to measure one's pulse?

_____

B Check whether the following statements are true or false.

1. The tongue is the most important muscle.   True ☐ False ☐

2. The heart pumping causes one's pulse to beat.   True ☐ False ☐

3. The heart has two chambers.   True ☐ False ☐

C Read and choose the best answers.

1. Which of the following is NOT part of the heart?

   a. chambers   b. ventricles   c. atria   d. lungs

2. Which of the following does blood carry to other parts of your body?

   a. muscles   b. food   c. oxygen   d. ventricles

3. What does your heart rate tell you?

   a. Which muscle is the strongest

   b. How much oxygen you are getting

   c. How fast your heart beats

   d. Where to put your fingers to find your pulse

4. Which of the following is true? **for NEAT**

   a. Richard did not know his heart was a muscle.

   b. The two sides of the heart perform the same function.

   c. The heart rests when you sleep.

   d. The atria are the bottom part of the heart.

A **Choose the best words to fill in the blanks.**

1. Researchers discovered a secret _____ full of treasure in the Great Pyramid.
   a. fist   b. chamber   c. pump   d. atria

2. When the doctor gave her the injection, she squeezed her _____ in pain.
   a. pulse   b. ventricles   c. lungs   d. fists

3. Even today, some people in remote areas _____ water from a well.
   a. pump   b. divide   c. beat   d. count

4. He _____ his waist in order to know what size pants to buy.
   a. worked   b. sent   c. felt   d. measured

B **Note the highlighted word in each selection. Then underline its synonym.**

1. Even though there is oxygen in the water, we can only breathe it as air.

2. The knight protected his chest with armor. This saved his life when the arrow failed to pierce his breast.

3. The child lacked the might to move the stone. She called her sister, who had more muscles than she did.

4. Miranda liked fast, upbeat rhythms, and the pulse of the music made her feel like dancing.

C **Match the appropriate meaning for the underlined word.**

> a. to move with a regular rhythm
>
> b. to defeat; win or be chosen over
>
> c. to strike repeated blows; hit repeatedly

1. A resting heart **beats** from 60 to 100 times a minute. _____

2. The child angrily **beat** his pillow with his fists. _____

3. Martial artists train long hours with the goal of **beating** their opponents. _____

Step 1. Summarizing

Fill in the blanks using words from the box below.

The heart is the most important muscle in the body. It is constantly _____. If it stops, even for a short while, it can be very _____ to the body. The heart's main function is to pump blood, which carries _____ from the lungs to other parts of the body. The heart has a left and a right side, each divided into top and bottom _____. The right side of the heart _____ blood to the lungs and the left side sends blood from the lungs out to the body. The top two chambers are called atria, while the bottom two are _____.

- ventricles
- oxygen
- dangerous
- beating
- chambers
- pumps

Step 2. Composition

How do you find your heart rate?

UNIT 05 60,000 Miles of Tubes

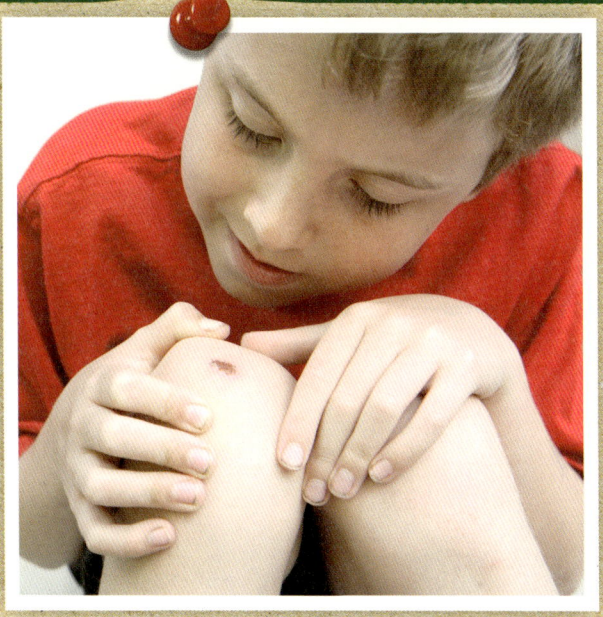

Subject: Science
Type: Lecture
Word Count: 293
Level of Difficulty: ★ ★ ★

Before You Read

• **Think about the following questions.**

1. What's the difference between an artery and a vein?

2. How many types of blood vessels are there?

Word Preview

• **Match the words to the correct definitions.**

1. _____ a tube in people, animals, or plants through which liquid flows; a large boat or ship

2. _____ a single unit of animal life or plant life. The human body is made of many kinds of cells.

3. _____ empty inside

4. _____ a force pressing on someone or something

5. 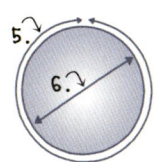   7. 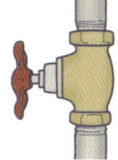   8.

5. _____   _____   _____

6. _____

circumference	valve	exchange	hollow	pressure
vessel	cell	diameter		

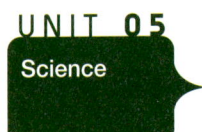
60,000 Miles of Tubes

Word Count: 293
Start time: _____
Finish time: _____
Reading time: _____

Reading strategies for fluent Reading

Intensive reading Intensive reading is used on shorter texts in order to extract specific information. It includes very close accurate reading for detail. Use intensive reading skills to grasp the details of a specific situation. In this case, it is important that you understand each word, number or fact.

1 Today we are going to study about blood vessels. Here is an amazing fact. If you could join together all the blood vessels in your body, they would stretch for about 60,000 miles! That's more than twice the circumference of the Earth! Now, the blood vessels in your body are all hollow tubes, but there are three different types
5 and they all do different things.

Arteries are the type of vessel that carry the blood away from your heart and take it to the rest of your body. The walls of arteries are thicker than the walls of the other blood vessels, because there is more pressure inside arteries than in the other blood vessels. The biggest artery is called the aorta, and it is about 2.5cm in
10 diameter.
Veins are the blood vessels that bring the blood back to the heart. Veins actually have valves inside them to make sure that blood cannot travel the wrong way. There are many more veins in your body than there are arteries, and at any given moment about 70% of your blood is in the veins.
15 The last type of blood vessel is called capillaries, and they are the smallest. The walls of the capillaries are very thin, and the capillaries are where the cells of the

● **Collocation builder**

stretch for to continue for a particular distance

body exchange oxygen in the blood with waste to be carried away. Capillaries join together the arteries and the veins.

So the process goes like this. Blood with lots of oxygen comes down the arteries
20 and into the capillaries. The capillaries give the oxygen to the cells in your body, and take waste back from the cells. The capillaries then pass this blood with the waste to the veins, and then the blood goes back to the heart.

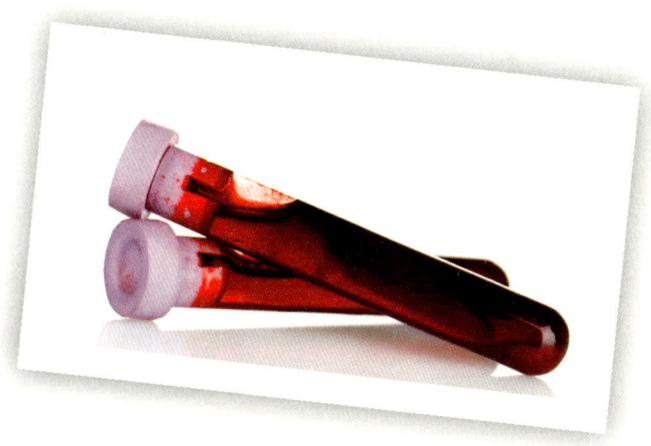

Skimming and Scanning Practice
Find where the following information is in the passage.

1. Oxygen-filled blood goes down the arteries into the capillaries.	Line _____
2. At any time, 70% of blood is contained in the veins.	Line _____
3. Artery walls are thicker than other blood vessel walls.	Line _____

Comprehension **Check-UP**

A > **Write the best answer.** **for NEAT**

1. What is the topic?

_____

2. What is the diameter of the aorta?

_____

B > **Check whether the following statements are true or false.**

1. Capillaries receive oxygen from cells in exchange for waste.   True ☐ False ☐

2. There are 60,000 miles of blood vessels in our bodies.   True ☐ False ☐

3. Capillaries are the biggest type of blood vessels.   True ☐ False ☐

C > **Read and choose the best answers.**

1. Which of the following is NOT one of the three types of blood vessels?

   a. aorta   b. capillary   c. artery   d. vein

2. Which of the following is something that only the capillaries do?

   a. Transport blood carrying waste back to the heart

   b. Contain 70% of your body's blood

   c. Exchange oxygen for waste with cells

   d. Bring oxygen from the heart to the arteries

3. Why are arteries the thickest type of blood vessel?

   a. They contain valves that control the direction of blood.

   b. They carry most of the blood in the body.

   c. They are the vessels that exchange with cells.

   d. They have more pressure than other blood vessels.

4. Which of the following is true? **for NEAT**

   a. There are more capillaries in the body than any other blood vessel.

   b. The aorta is the smallest artery in the body.

   c. Veins are the blood vessels that link capillaries to arteries

   d. Valves in veins prevent blood from flowing the wrong way.

36

Word Power-UP

A Choose the best words to fill in the blanks.

1. A single _____ can contain all that is necessary for life.
   a. capillary   b. blood vessel   c. exchange   d. cell

2. When mom gets angry, the _____ in her forehead get bigger.
   a. wastes   b. bodies   c. veins   d. valves

3. The shipping _____ carried cargo from Asia to Europe.
   a. hollow   b. vessel   c. valve   d. vein

4. I have to replace the _____ in my faucet to fix the leak.
   a. diameter   b. cell   c. pressure   d. valve

B Note the highlighted word in each selection. Then underline its synonym.

1. Do you know the earth's circumference? Ancient Greek mathematicians figured out the perimeter in 200 B.C.

2. Submarines must withstand intense pressure. The deeper they go, the stronger the force upon them is.

3. Unlike our bones, bird bones are hollow. Because they are empty, they are lighter.

4. The shirt that George bought didn't fit so he went to exchange it. He traded it for one that fit better.

C Match the right meaning as the underlined words.

> a. to continue for a particular distance
>
> b. to make your arms, legs, or body as straight as possible
>
> c. a continuous period of time

1. Stretching before working out can help to prevent injury. _____

2. My father spends long stretches of time traveling for work. _____

3. The fields of corn stretched for as far as the eye could see. _____

Sum UP! Review & Finalize

Summarizing

Complete the diagram with the words from the box below.

<u>Introduction</u>

Our bodies are full of many small tubes, called blood vessels, which move blood around our body. There are three different types of blood vessels: arteries, veins, and _____.

<u>Arteries</u>

Because they handle more _____ than other vessels, arteries are the thickest of the blood vessels. They are responsible for bringing blood filled with oxygen from the heart out to different parts of the body.

<u>Veins</u>

Veins are most common type of blood vessel. 70% of our blood is in our veins. They bring blood carrying cellular _____ back to the heart.

<u>Capillaries</u>

The _____ of the blood vessels, capillaries, connect the arteries to the veins. They take oxygen and _____ it for waste from cells. Then they pass the blood on to the veins.

<u>Conclusion</u>

The different types of blood _____ have different jobs to do, and they all work together to do a very important job, keeping us alive!

▪ smallest	▪ pressure	▪ vessels	▪ exchange	▪ capillaries
▪ waste				

Subject: Science
Type: Letter
Word Count: 251
Level of Difficulty: ★★★★

Before You Read

• **Think about the following questions.**

1. What is H_2O?

2. What language does the word 'atom' come from?

Word Preview

• **Match the words to the correct definitions.**

1. _____ the smallest unit of any substance.

2. _____ to join one thing to another

3. _____ a gas that has no color or smell and is lighter than air

4. _____ the smallest part of an element. It consists of two or more atoms.

5. _____ relating to the use of an electric current to produce a magnetic field

| molecule | attach | atom | hydrogen | electromagnetic |

UNIT 06

Science **Atoms**

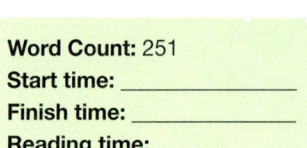

Word Count: 251
Start time: _____
Finish time: _____
Reading time: _____

Reading strategies for fluent Reading

Extensive reading Extensive reading is used to obtain a general understanding of a subject and includes reading longer texts for pleasure. Use extensive reading skills to improve your general knowledge. Do not worry if you don't understand each word.

1 Dear Gareth,

I'm sorry I have not written for a while, so here's a present for you. I've attached a piece of my hair to this page; so actually I'm giving you millions of presents. Do you know why?

5 My present to you is atoms! And atoms are so small that there are millions of them just in this piece of hair. There are about 100,000 of them just in the width of my hair, and that hair is 10cm long!

Do you know about atoms? They are the basic unit of matter and everything is made from them, from the stars in the sky to the soap in your bathroom. There 10 are lots of different types of atoms, and something called a hydrogen atom is the smallest, while something like an oxygen atom is bigger, but is still far too small to see. Now, different atoms can join together to form something else, and two different atoms joined together are called molecules. You know water is sometimes called H_2O. This is because water is a molecule that has two hydrogen 15 atoms joined to one oxygen atom by something called electromagnetic force.

 **Collocation builder**

look up to find information by looking in a book or using a computer

I looked up why they are called atoms. The name comes from a Greek word, 'atomos,' which means 'something that cannot be divided further.' They called it this because at the time they thought atoms were the smallest things in the world.

I promise to send you a proper present next time! Please write to me soon.

Love,
Louis

Skimming and Scanning Practice
Find where the following information is in the passage.

1. A molecule is made up of atoms that are connected together.	Line _____
2. Atoms are so tiny that a single hair contains millions of them.	Line _____
3. They named it that believing that nothing could be smaller than an atom.	Line _____

Comprehension Check-UP

A **Write the best answer.** for NEAT

1. What is the topic?

_____

2. What keeps atoms joined together to form molecules?

_____

B **Check whether the following statements are true or false.**

1. Soap has the same number of atoms as a star.   True ☐ False ☐

2. Water is made with one oxygen and two hydrogen atoms.   True ☐ False ☐

3. 'Atomos' is Greek for 'dividing something further.'   True ☐ False ☐

C **Read and choose the best answers.**

1. Which of the following is NOT made up of atoms?

   a. electromagnetic force   b. stars

   c. water molecules   d. hair

2. Which of the following is formed by joining atoms?

   a. proper presents

   b. molecules

   c. basic units of matter

   d. electromagnetic force

3. Which of the following was NOT mentioned in the letter?

   a. The origin of the word 'molecule'

   b. The difference between oxygen and hydrogen atoms

   c. The amount of atoms a piece of hair contains

   d. How atoms are joined together

4. Which of the following is true? for NEAT

   a. A piece of hair has 100,000 atoms.

   b. We cannot actually see atoms.

   c. Stars contain water molecules.

   d. Hydrogen atoms are bigger than oxygen atoms

A **Choose the best words to fill in the blanks.**

1. Alex didn't like the birthday _____ his grandmother gave him, but he thanked her anyways.

   a. form   b. hair   c. promise   d. present

2. The _____ of Ethan's feet made it difficult to find shoes that fit.

   a. page   b. force   c. width   d. piece

3. While bathing her baby, the woman was careful not to get _____ in his eyes.

   a. oxygen   b. atom   c. soap   d. basic

4. Engineers can change one _____ into another by removing or adding an atom.

   a. electromagnetic   b. word   c. hydrogen   d. molecule

B **Note the highlighted word in each selection. Then underline its synonym.**

1. It's not appropriate to speak while chewing food. Many people don't seem to have these proper manners.

2. She attached a picture of herself in the e-mail and linked to her website.

3. Ellen promised to take care of her friend's cat. She guaranteed it would live a happy life.

4. Karen started learning basic Arabic but the fundamental grammar already seems too difficult.

C **Match the right meaning as the underlined words.**

> a. a subject, topic, or problem
>
> b. the physical world made up of atoms
>
> c. to have meaning or significance

1. Sometimes having a good attitude **matters** more than one's ability. _____

2. After agreeing on the schedule they began discussing the **matter** of money. _____

3. According to Einstein's theory, **matter** is energy that has been frozen solid. _____

Summarizing

Complete the diagram with the words from the box below.

Introduction

What are atoms? Atoms are the basic unit of _____ and form everything in the material world. A single piece of _____ contains millions of atoms.

Origin of the word

The world atom comes from the Greek word, 'atomos,' which means 'something that cannot be divided _____.' It cannot be broken into any smaller pieces.

Molecules

The smallest type of atoms are _____ atoms. When two hydrogen atoms are combined with one oxygen atom, a water _____ is formed. Different combinations of different atoms will create other kinds of molecules.

Electromagnetic force

What makes atoms join together? The _____ that holds these atoms together as a molecule is called electromagnetic force.

Conclusion

Everything in the universe, from stars to soap, is made up of atoms. As these atoms are rearranged the world also changes.

- hydrogen   - force   - molecule   - hair   - further
- matter

Subject: Science
Type: Conversation
Word Count: 254
Level of Difficulty: ★ ★ ★ ★ ★

Before You Read

• **Think about the following questions.**

1. What is the nucleus of an atom?

2. What does an atom look like?

Word Preview

• **Match the words to the correct definitions.**

1. _____ very firmly or strongly

2. _____ a small round mark or spot

3. _____ working by electricity

4. _____ to move around a large object in space such as a planet; to make a circular movement around the nucleus of an atom

5. _____ the central or basic part of something; the central part of an atom

6. _____ to fill a place completely

| nucleus | orbit | electrical | dot | tightly | pack |

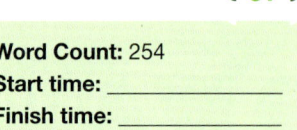

What's inside an Atom?

Word Count: 254
Start time: _____
Finish time: _____
Reading time: _____

Reading strategies for fluent Reading

Scanning Scanning is used to find a particular piece of information. Run your eyes over the text looking for the specific piece of information you need. Use scanning on schedules, meeting plans, etc. in order to find the specific details you require. If you see words or phrases that you don't understand, don't worry when scanning.

1 Scarlet: An atom is the smallest thing in the whole world.

Adrian: No, it's not. There are things inside atoms, called particles.

Scarlet: No! Atoms are the things that make everything in the whole universe. A tin can is made of billions and billions of tin atoms. And atoms can join
5 together to make molecules, and molecules make everything from trees to tables to human beings.

Adrian: Well, you're right, but actually there are very small particles that make an atom. Here, let's look on the Internet.

"Atoms are made from three types of tiny particles, called protons, neutrons,
10 and electrons. Imagine a circle with a very small dot in the center. This looks like an atom. The small dot in the center is called the nucleus of the atom. Inside the nucleus are the protons and the neutrons, packed tightly together. A proton has

a positive electrical charge. A neutron does not have any electrical charge. The circumference of the circle we imagined is just like the outer part of the

15 atom. Here, electrons travel around; orbiting the nucleus of the atom just like the moon orbits the Earth. These electrons have a negative electrical charge and are much smaller than protons. An atom will have the same number of electrons as protons."

Adrian: So you see, there are things inside atoms. My science teacher says that
20 actually there are probably things inside protons and neutrons, called quarks.

Scarlet: Well, I suppose you learn something new every day. An atom isn't the smallest thing in the whole world!

● **Skimming and Scanning Practice**
Find where the following information is in the passage.

1. Electrons orbit an atom's nucleus similar to the moon around the Earth.	Line _____
2. Something called quarks likely exists inside protons and neutrons.	Line _____
3. In an atom, the number of protons matches that of electrons.	Line _____

Comprehension Check-UP

A **Write the best answer.** for NEAT

1. What is the topic?

_____

2. What did Scarlet learn in the passage?

_____

B **Check whether the following statements are true or false.**

1. The moon is an electron.   True ☐   False ☐

2. Atoms are the smallest thing in the world.   True ☐   False ☐

3. Electrons are smaller than protons.   True ☐   False ☐

C **Read and choose the best answers.**

1. Which of the following makes up the nucleus of an atom?

   a. The nucleus is actually full of empty space.

   b. Negative electrons and quarks

   c. Negative neutrons and positive protons

   d. Neutral neutrons and positive protons

2. What do protons and electrons have in common?

   a. There is the same number of each in an atom.

   b. They are the same size.

   c. They both have negative charges.

   d. There are twice as many as them as neutrons.

3. Which of the following is true? for NEAT

   a. Some molecules don't have a nucleus.

   b. Neutrons are smaller than protons.

   c. Quarks are even smaller than electrons.

   d. Electrons are at the center of an atom.

A Choose the best words to fill in the blanks.

1. Along with protons, _____ make up the nucleus of an atom.
     a. dots   b. charges   c. electrons   d. neutrons

2. During a lightning storm, an electrical _____ is delivered from a cloud to the earth.
     a. orbit   b. charge   c. dot   d. proton

3. Paul's bag was _____ with snacks and toys to share with his nephews and nieces.
     a. joined   b. played   c. supposed   d. packed

4. Now that the rain has stopped, I _____ we can continue our soccer game.
     a. join   b. play   c. quark   d. suppose

B Note the highlighted word in each selection. Then underline its synonym.

1. Every company has a nucleus of essential workers. This team is that core for our company.

2. Just as the Earth orbits the sun, the moon is circling around the planet.

3. Some mushrooms have spots and others don't. The one I'm looking for has white dots on it.

4. Until today, their marriage was a tightly held secret. Reporters will be watching closely for details.

C Match the right meaning as the underlined words.

> a. the amount or type of electrical force
>
> b. to ask (a given amount) as a price
>
> c. to make a claim of wrongdoing against; blame

1. The man was **charged** with careless driving and ignoring traffic laws. _____

2. The clerk **charged** her five dollars for the magazines. _____

3. Magnets with opposite **charges** are attracted together. _____

Step 1. Summarizing

Fill in the blanks using words from the box below.

Is there anything smaller than an atom? In fact, there is. Those are the _____ that make up the atom itself. An atom consists of a central part, called a nucleus, and an outer ring-shaped part that _____ it, where electrons move. The _____ has two parts, protons and neutrons. Protons have a positive _____, while neutrons don't have any. Electrons, which are much smaller than protons and neutrons, have a _____ charge. Interestingly, an atom always has the same amount of protons as it does electrons. Scientists think that these particles are made up of even tinier parts, known as _____. It seems there's no end to the mysteries of science!

- negative   - nucleus   - charge   - quarks   - particles
- orbits

Step 2. Composition

What is the smallest thing in the world?

UNIT 08 How the Wind Blows

Subject: Science
Type: Lecture
Word Count: 250
Level of Difficulty: ★ ★ ★

Before You Read

• **Think about the following questions.**

1. Why does the wind blow?
2. What part of the earth has the warmest air?

Word Preview

• **Match the words to the correct definitions.**

1. _____ a light wind

2. _____ a very strong wind

3. _____ having parts very close together with little space between

4. _____ to open or stretch wide

5. _____ to move to a lower level

6.

_____

the Equator	dense	spread	gale	breeze	sink

How the Wind Blows

Word Count: 250
Start time: _____
Finish time: _____
Reading time: _____

Reading strategies for fluent Reading

Skimming Skimming is looking quickly through the text to get a general idea of what it is about. We move our eyes quickly through the whole text, allowing us to identify the purpose of the passage or the main idea.

1 Today's guest is A. E. Passmore, and he is here to talk about the wind.

"Good morning, children. Have you ever wondered what makes the wind? You might be surprised that the Sun has a lot to do with it!

Different parts of the Earth get different amounts of heat from the Sun. The
5 Equator is the line running around the center of the Earth, and places close to the Equator get the most heat. On the other hand, the North and South Poles of the Earth get the least amount of heat, so the air there stays the coolest. Now, most of you probably know that hot air rises, and cold air sinks. So, the warmer air from above the Equator spreads up and gets less dense — and we call this a *low-*
10 *pressure air system*. This air moves towards the cooler, denser air by the North and South Poles. The cooler air is called a *high-pressure air system*, and it moves towards the Equator. Of course, once a high-pressure system gets to the Equator it gets more heat from the Sun. It then gets warmer, turns into a low-pressure system and travels towards the Poles again. This cycle continues over and over, creating
15 wind.

● Collocation builder

have to do with   to be connected with someone or something

over and over   many times

Lastly, there are different types of wind. A breeze is wind traveling between 10 to 20 miles per hour. If wind travels 40 to 50 miles per hour it is a gale, and if it goes over 75 miles per hour it is a hurricane."

Skimming and Scanning Practice
Find where the following information is in the passage.

1. Cooler air, called a high-pressure system, moves towards the Equator.　Line _____

2. The Sun is one of the most important factors in making wind.　Line _____

3. The places near the Equator, the line around the center of the Earth, are the hottest.

Line _____

Comprehension Check-UP

A **Write the best answer.** **for NEAT**

1. What is the topic?

_____

2. What part of the Earth gets the least heat from the sun?

_____

B **Check whether the following statements are true or false.**

1. A gale is the slowest type of wind.   True ☐   False ☐

2. Hot air rises and cold air sinks.   True ☐   False ☐

3. Low-pressure air systems start at the poles.   True ☐   False ☐

C **Read and choose the best answers.**

1. Which of the following is NOT explained in the presentation?

   a. Why wind has different speeds

   b. What makes wind

   c. How temperature affects air systems

   d. The difference between high and low-pressure systems

2. Which of the following runs around the center of the Earth?

   a. hurricanes   b. cold air

   c. low-pressure air systems   d. the Equator

3. How does the Sun help to make wind?

   a. The gravity from the Sun affects the air pressure system.

   b. By warming up the air more in one part of the Earth than another

   c. Solar winds come off the Sun and create wind on Earth.

   d. The Sun is not a factor in making wind.

4. Which of the following is true? **for NEAT**

   a. Air all over the world is the same temperature.

   b. A breeze blows at 30 miles per hour.

   c. Cooler air moves towards the poles.

   d. The air sinks in high-pressure systems.

A Choose the best words to fill in the blanks.

1. Samantha was nervous because it was her first time _____ by plane.
   a. spreading   b. traveling   c. sinking   d. heating

2. Using the solar energy is a cheap and clean way to _____ buildings.
   a. spread   b. gale   c. heat   d. center

3. The _____ of the apple had been eaten by insects.
   a. heat   b. Equator   c. breeze   d. center

4. Were you _____ to get first place in the contest?
   a. surprised   b. wondered   c. created   d. closed

B Note the highlighted word in each selection. Then underline its synonym.

1. After a breeze knocked over the vase, Terry blocked the wind by closing the window.

2. While the heart of a city is extremely compact, the suburbs are much less dense in population.

3. Psy's music spread throughout the Internet, his popularity greatly expanded.

4. A large quantity of food takes a bigger amount of time to prepare.

C Match the right meaning as the underlined words.

> a. to doubt
>
> b. something strange and surprising; a cause of surprise or admiration
>
> c. to be curious to know

1. Snowboarding is so difficult, it's a **wonder** that he didn't once fall down. _____

2. Have you ever **wondered** what it would be like to live in another country? _____

3. I **wonder** if he'll actually finish his work in time for class. _____

Step 1. Sentence Completion

Draw a line between A and B to complete each sentence.

A

1. First, warm air rises as a low-pressure system

2. This cycle of air from the Equator

3. Because of the Sun, the Equator

4. Then, air at the Poles becomes high-pressure systems

5. Surprisingly, the Sun has a lot to do

B

a. is hot while the Poles are cooler.

b. with the making of wind.

c. and moves to the Poles.

d. to the Poles is wind.

e. and move back to the Equator.

Step 2. Sequencing

Put the sentences in the correct order.

How Wind Is Formed

1. _____

2. _____

3. _____

4. _____

5. _____

UNIT 09 Let's Be Cartographers!

Subject: Geoscience
Type: Presentation
Word Count: 293
Level of Difficulty: ★ ★ ★ ★

Before You Read

• **Think about the following questions.**

1. What does a cartographer do?

2. What is the line that travels around the center of the Earth?

Word Preview

• **Match the words to the correct definitions.**

1. _____ not real but only created in your mind

2. _____ an extremely large group of stars and planets

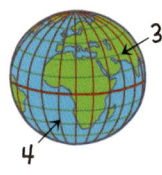

5.

6. 1)

2) similar and happening at the same time

3. _____   _____   _____

4. _____

galaxy	longitude	coordinate	imaginary	parallel
latitude				

Let's Be Cartographers!

Track
09

Word Count: 293
Start time: _____
Finish time: _____
Reading time: _____

Reading strategies for fluent Reading

Identifying time order Writers often use dates and times, or other words, to show the order of events – for example, first, next, then, later, finally, and today. These words can help you to understand a passage better. Read carefully and identify those words.

1 Hello ladies and gentlemen, my name is Lucy, and today I am going to talk to you about maps.

You all know that a map is a drawing that shows people what is in a particular area. When most people think about a map they think of the map of their country,
5 or of a map of the whole world. But remember, a map can show what is in any type of area, so there are maps of space that show where all the galaxies are, and there are even maps of all the blood vessels in our body.

So, have you ever been a cartographer? I bet you have even if you do not know what a cartographer is! If you've ever drawn a picture to show your friend how to
10 get to your house, you've drawn a type of map. Your picture shows what is in the area around your house so that your friend can find your house, so it is a map. And a person that draws a map is a cartographer.

After my presentation today, we are going to be cartographers and draw a map of the whole world.

15 When we draw our maps of the world, we must remember to include some important lines on our maps. The imaginary line that goes around the middle of the Earth is called the Equator. We need to draw parallel lines to the north and the south of the Equator, and these are called lines of latitude. We must also draw lines from the North Pole to the South Pole, and these are called the lines of longitude.

20 The point where a line of longitude and latitude meet is called a coordinate.

Now, let's be cartographers and draw our maps!

Skimming and Scanning Practice
Find where the following information is in the passage.

1. If you draw a world map, there are some important lines that must be included.

Line _____

2. There are maps that show all of our blood vessels or even where galaxies are.

Line _____

3. When you draw a picture showing your friend where your house is, it will include what is around your house.

Line _____

Comprehension Check-UP

A Write the best answer. **for NEAT**

1. What is the topic?

_____

2. What is a coordinate?

_____

B Check whether the following statements are true or false.

1. Lines of longitude run parallel to the Equator. True ☐ False ☐

2. Cartographers are people who draw maps. True ☐ False ☐

3. The Equator is an imaginary line. True ☐ False ☐

C Read and choose the best answers.

1. Which of the following is NOT a map mentioned in the passage?

   a. a map of the way to your house   b. a map of the library

   c. a map of blood vessels   d. a map of outer space

2. Which of the following means that someone is a cartographer?

   a. Being able to read a map

   b. Determining the coordinates of a location

   c. Drawing a picture of the way to your house

   d. Knowing the difference between latitude and longitude

3. How can a drawing of blood vessels be considered as a map?

   a. It has imaginary lines that tell us where to go.

   b. It shows what is in a certain area.

   c. It is something that we can draw.

   d. Doctors are also cartographers.

4. Which of the following is true? **for NEAT**

   a. Maps are only for countries and the world.

   b. The students are going to draw a map to their house.

   c. Coordinates are imaginary lines that run from the North to South Pole.

   d. We need to know the latitude and longitude to find a coordinate.

A Choose the best words to fill in the blanks.

1. Some people are better at reading _____ than others when finding the way.
   a. paper   b. maps   c. lines   d. middle

2. I _____ I'll get a better score than you on the today's test.
   a. coordinate   b. think   c. draw   d. bet

3. Ancient _____ used to draw the earth as a flat world.
   a. gentlemen   b. cartographers c. galaxies   d. doctors

4. Lines of latitude run _____ to the Equator.
   a. particular   b. whole   c. parallel   d. around

B Note the highlighted word in each selection. Then underline its synonym.

1. He wasn't sure of his exact location, so he used a map to determine his coordinates.

2. The unicorn is a well-known nonexistent animal. People seem to be fascinated by imaginary creatures.

3. Many galaxies take a spiral form. Some star systems, however, are more irregularly shaped.

4. Due to their similar histories, the two countries also shared parallel interests.

C Match the right meaning as the underlined words.

> a. to choose things to look good together
>
> b. any of a set of numbers that defines the location of a point in space
>
> c. balanced; to control the movements of different parts of your body
>
> d. to organize the different parts of a job

1. Not being very **coordinated**, I fall down whenever I ice skate. _____

2. The ship gave their **coordinates** so that they could be rescued. _____

3. I tried to **coordinate** my clothes so that they go well together. _____

4. The three countries are working together to **coordinate** policies. _____

Step 1. Summarizing

Fill in the blanks using words from the box below.

Have you ever drawn a map? People who make maps are called _____.
Maps can be about many things, countries, _____, even parts of our body. If it
gives visual information about a certain area, it can be called a map. Maps of the world,
however, contain important lines that help us to understand the distance and location of
places. The _____ line that runs around the middle of the Earth is the Equator.
Lines of latitude run parallel to the _____ to the north and south. Lines of
_____ run from the North to the South pole. The points where these lines meet is
called a _____.

- imaginary
- Equator
- galaxies
- cartographers
- coordinate
- longitude

Step 2. Composition

When might someone have to draw a map?

Subject: Geoscience
Type: Letter
Word Count: 283
Level of Difficulty: ★

Before You Read

• **Think about the following questions.**

1. In which US region are orange orchards common?
2. Can you name a large Midwest city?

Word Preview

• **Match the words to the correct definitions.**

1. _____ to make or grow something

2. _____ the study of the countries, oceans, rivers, mountains, cities etc of the world

3. _____ to be next to another country or region; the official line separating two countries or states

4. _____ a large area of a country or of the world

5. _____ a tall plant that produces grain for making bread and other foods

| region | wheat | border | geography | produce |

So Different!

Word Count: 283
Start time: _____
Finish time: _____
Reading time: _____

Reading strategies for fluent Reading

Understanding the details Details give readers a better explanation of what the author is trying to say. Details could be used to further describe the topic or to give examples. When dealing with detail questions, only use the information given in the text. Do not imply.

1 Hi Paul, this is Tom. I'm sorry I haven't sent you any emails lately, but I've been studying really hard for my exams. I had my geography exam yesterday. It was about the different regions of the United States of America. I was happy when I saw the exam paper because I know lots about America!

5 Although there are 50 states in America, there are only eight regions. The *Northwest* region is close to Canada and is bordered by the Pacific Ocean. It gets lots of rain. The *Southwest* region is also bordered by the Pacific Ocean. The Grand Canyon and the Colorado River are in the Southwest region.

The *West* region has the Rocky Mountains as well as Death Valley. Death Valley is 10 so hot and dry that hardly anything can live there.

There is a region called the *Great Plains* and a region called the *Midwest*. Both of these regions are famous for farming, especially corn, wheat, and soybeans. However, not many people live in the Great Plains but lots of people live in the Midwest because it has cities such as Chicago and Cleveland. The Midwest also

¹⁵ has the Great Lakes.

In the *South* region winters are not too bad. That's why it has lots of farms that produce things like oranges in Florida and peaches in Georgia.

The *Mid-Atlantic* region is bordered by the Atlantic Ocean and this region has lots of people in cities such as Washington, D.C., New York and Philadelphia.

²⁰ In the top corner of the US is the region called *New England*. It is very famous for the way the leaves change color in the fall.

Please email me about the regions of your country!

Skimming and Scanning Practice
Find where the following information is in the passage.

1. Being quite familiar with the United States, I was happy when I saw the test paper.

Line _____

2. Hardly anything can live in Death Valley because it is so dry and hot.   Line _____

3. New England is known for the leaves changing colors in fall.   Line _____

A **Write the best answer.** `for NEAT`

1. What is the topic?

_____

2. Why was the author happy to see the exam paper?

_____

B **Check whether the following statements are true or false.**

1. Georgia is famous for producing peaches.　　　　　　　　　True ☐　False ☐

2. The Northwest region is bordered by the Atlantic Ocean.　　True ☐　False ☐

3. The United States has a total of 52 states.　　　　　　　　　True ☐　False ☐

C **Read and choose the best answers.**

1. Which of the following is NOT the name of a region of the United States?

　a. Northwest　　　　b. South　　　　c. Northeast　　　　d. New England

2. Which of the following is one reason many people live in the Midwest?

　a. Large cities like Chicago are located there.

　b. Because there is so much space for people to live.

　c. Lots of farms give people plenty of food and jobs.

　d. People want to live near the Great Lakes.

3. What do the Midwest and the Great Plains regions share together?

　a. The Great Lakes

　b. Large cities

　c. Both border the Pacific Ocean.

　d. Lots of farmland

4. Which of the following is true? `for NEAT`

　a. Winters are especially cold in the South.

　b. Death Valley is in the same region as the Rocky Mountains.

　c. The West is where the Grand Canyon is located.

　d. England is a region in the United States.

Word Power-UP

A   Choose the best words to fill in the blanks.

1. During the game of hide and seek, Kevin went to hide in the _____ of the room.

   a. corner   b. border   c. Midwest   d. outside

2. *Tofu*, a cake-like food made of _____, is quite popular among vegetarians.

   a. produce   b. leaves   c. wheat   d. soybean

3. Some people are allergic to _____, meaning that they can't eat bread and noodles.

   a. farms   b. produce   c. geography   d. wheat

4. Students of _____ study not only the physical earth, but also human society.

   a. regions   b. geography   c. borders   d. math

B   Note the highlighted word in each selection. Then underline its synonym.

1. I'm looking for an area suited for stargazing. Perhaps a desert region would be ideal.

2. The US-Canada boundary is quite relaxed. It's not so difficult to cross the border there.

3. Businesses should manufacture products cheaply and in order to produce profits.

4. What have you been up to lately? We haven't seen much of you these days.

C   Match the right meaning as the underlined words.

> a. fruit, vegetables, and other things that farmers grow
>
> b. to make or grow something
>
> c. to show or offer something

1. You must **produce** documents proving you are a student to get the discount. _____

2. **Produce** is fresher at a farmer's market because it is grown locally. _____

3. Wisconsin is famous for **producing** cheese. _____

Summarizing

Complete the diagram with the words from the box below.

The 8 Regions of the US

Northwest	close to Canada, bordered by the Pacific Ocean, gets lots of _____
Southwest	bordered by the Pacific, contains the Grand Canyon and _____ River
West	has the Rocky Mountains and Death Valley (extremely hot and dry)
Great Plains	farming of corn, wheat, soybeans, and few people live here
Midwest	also has farming of corn, wheat, soybeans, but many people in _____ like Chicago and Cleveland, Great Lakes
South	_____ winters, farms, Florida oranges, Georgia peaches
Mid-Atlantic	_____ by the Atlantic Ocean, has large cities like Washington, D.C., New York and Philadelphia
New England	top _____ of the US, famous for its fall leaf colors

- mild
- corner
- rain
- Colorado
- cities
- bordered

UNIT
11 After the Roman Empire

Subject: History
Type: Letter
Word Count: 288
Level of Difficulty: ★ ★ ★

Before You Read

• **Think about the following questions.**

1. Why did the Roman Empire collapse?

2. What does 'medieval' mean?

Word Preview

• **Match the words to the correct definitions.**

1. _____ always or regularly

2. _____ to damage; ruin

3. _____ the situation of being poor

4. _____ if a system collapses, it suddenly fails; to fall down suddenly; a sudden failure

5. _____ a period of 100 years

6. _____ to get control of a country by fighting

7. _____ to gradually affect a larger area

8. _____ to be all over a surface

9. _____ extremely large in size

10. _____ a large group of related families who live in the same area and share a common language, religion, and customs

spread	huge	century	tribe	collapse	destroy
constantly	poverty	conquer	cover		

After the Roman Empire

Track 11

Word Count: 288
Start time: _____
Finish time: _____
Reading time: _____

Reading strategies for fluent Reading

Guessing unknown words in context We often meet unknown words while reading a passage. At that time, context gives us an idea of the possible meaning. We can also use our knowledge of how a word is put together to work out its meaning.

1 Hi Darren, how are you?

Isn't it amazing that I can sit here and write an email to you? Things were very different in the Middle Ages in Europe.

Apparently, the Middle Ages were around the middle of the 5th century to around
5 the middle of the 15th century. It was the period of history after the Roman Empire had collapsed. I never realized how big the Roman Empire was, but it actually covered places as far apart as Spain, England, Greece, Egypt, Northern Africa and the Middle East. But this huge Empire became so big that it was too difficult to manage, and various tribes of people from Europe and Asia began to conquer
10 parts of the Empire. There were the Vandals that conquered Italy, the Huns from Northern China and Russia who spread into much of Europe, and there were two tribes that conquered England, called the Angles and the Saxons. So eventually the Roman Empire collapsed, and Europe entered the 'Middle Ages.' You may have seen the word 'medieval,' and this refers to the Middle Ages.

● **Collocation builder**

far apart not close to each other

may have p.p. used for talking about past possibilities

refer to to describe something, or to be about something

15 After the Roman Empire had collapsed, life in Europe was very difficult. The different tribes were constantly fighting, the Roman cities and buildings were destroyed, and trade with other areas became much more difficult. People lived in poverty, had to work extremely hard just to survive, and usually died at a very young age. Another term you may have heard is the 'Dark Ages,' and this term

20 refers to the first 3 hundred years (476–800) after the collapse of the Roman Empire, because people thought that things were very bad in Europe during that time.

I have to go to soccer practice now. I'll email you again soon.

Skimming and Scanning Practice
Find where the following information is in the passage.

1. During the Middle Ages, living conditions were very poor, and people worked hard to survive

Line _____

2. Different European and Asian tribes started to conquer parts of the Roman Empire.

Line _____

3. Ultimately, the Roman Empire fell and Europe began the Middle Ages.   Line _____

Comprehension Check-UP

A Write the best answer. for NEAT

1. What is the topic?

_____

2. Which tribe conquered Italy after the fall of Rome?

_____

B Check whether the following statements are true or false.

1. The Middle Ages lasted around one thousand years.   True ☐   False ☐

2. The Roman Empire included parts of Africa.   True ☐   False ☐

3. The Huns succeeded in conquering England.   True ☐   False ☐

C Read and choose the best answers.

1. Which of the following terms describes the years 476–800?

   a. the medieval period   b. the Black Times

   c. the Middle Ages   d. the Dark Ages

2. Which of the following tribes conquered England?

   a. The Saxons   b. The Vandals

   c. The Russians   d. The Huns

3. Which of the following factors influenced the Roman Empire's collapse?

   a. There were too many different cultures in the Empire.

   b. With one big Empire, there was nobody to fight.

   c. Its large size made it difficult to manage.

   d. Its economy helped to strengthen its enemies.

4. Which of the following is true? for NEAT

   a. The Roman Empire was only in Europe.

   b. Trade increased during the Dark Ages.

   c. The Middle Ages ended in the 9th century.

   d. Elderly people were rare during the Dark Ages.

A Choose the best words to fill in the blanks.

1. Chickenpox is an itchy skin disease that can _____ all over your body.

   a. fight   b. spread   c. collapse   d. destroy

2. When people talk about the 21st _____ they are referring to the years 2001-2100.

   a. century   b. cover   c. tribe   d. poverty

3. After _____ receiving phone calls from reporters, she decided to turn her phone off.

   a. apparently   b. actually   c. eventually   d. constantly

4. Similar to humans, apes will form _____ that live together in a certain territory.

   a. empires   b. covers   c. centuries   d. tribes

B Note the highlighted word in each selection. Then underline its synonym.

1. The director spent a huge amount of money and hoped the film would be a giant success.

2. If the economy crashes, it will mean the collapse of many businesses.

3. Poorness is quite serious in some countries. Those who can need to help fight extreme poverty.

4. My father conquered his fear of flying. He overcame his phobia so he could travel with us.

C Match the right meaning as the underlined words.

> a. to place something over
>
> b. a blanket, quilt, or the like
>
> c. to report the details of an event for a newspaper or a television

1. After washing the bed **covers**, he hung them up to dry on the clothesline. _____

2. It's polite to **cover** your mouth with your hand when you sneeze. _____

3. The soccer team's amazing victory was **covered** by the international press. _____

Step 1. Sentence Completion

Draw a line between A and B to complete each sentence.

A

1. After the Empire collapsed,

2. The Middle Ages lasted between

3. There was constant fighting, trade was difficult,

4. This era began with the fall

5. The Roman Empire was difficult to manage

B

a. and people died young.

b. and under attack by outsiders.

c. of the Roman Empire.

d. the 5th and the 15th centuries.

e. Europe fell into chaos.

Step 2. Sequencing

Put the sentences in the correct order.

> **After the Fall of Rome**

1. _____

2. _____

3. _____

4. _____

5. _____

UNIT 12 Not So Dark After All

Subject: History
Type: Expository essay
Word Count: 279
Level of Difficulty: ★ ★ ★ ★

Before You Read

• **Think about the following questions.**

1. Where did the term 'Dark Ages' come from?
2. What is a feudal system?

Word Preview

• **Match the words to the correct definitions.**

1. _____ an amount of money that you must pay to the government

2. _____ to protect yourself against the risk of something

3. _____ books, plays, poems etc

4. _____ to make something better, or to become better

5. _____ to do a job or to perform duties for a person or organization

6. _____ a man in medieval Europe who was very powerful and owned a lot of land

7. _____ a poor farmer who owns or rents a small amount of land (= serf)

8.

9.

_____   _____

literature	improve	serve	lord	peasant	cathedral
ensure	knight	tax			

Not So Dark After All

Word Count: 279
Start time: _____
Finish time: _____
Reading time: _____

Track
12

Reading strategies for fluent Reading

Making inferences Making inferences means understanding something that is not mentioned directly. Whenever we read, we can assume certain things from the information we learn. But we must be careful not to assume too much. Everything we "infer" must be based on the information given.

1 In the 1300s, an Italian poet called Petrarch thought that nothing good had happened in Europe right after the Roman Empire had collapsed, so he called the period between the 5th and 8th centuries the 'Dark Ages.' But actually, maybe they were not so dark.

5 Although life was tough, this period in history saw the development of many things. The Roman Catholic Church grew stronger, and became the center of learning, knowledge, and development. The church kept books, it collected taxes, it built huge churches and cathedrals, and it became the center of many people's lives. Most people could not read or write, and the church was the place that
10 ensured classic literature and even the Bible survived.

Also, the 'Dark Ages' saw the development of the Feudal system. A king was supported by powerful people, called lords. These lords gave land to people, who in return promised to serve the lord. The person who received the land was called a vassal, and if a lord had lots of vassals he could become powerful. Knights were
15 the soldiers who served the lords and kings, and they fought whenever the lord or

● Collocation builder

in return as payment or in exchange for something

king needed help, and got paid with land or money. Peasants, or serfs, were the people who worked on the farms owned by the lords. Although life was still hard, this system developed and eventually powerful lords created towns and kingdoms, and life for most people started to improve. These kingdoms later developed into

20 the countries we know today as the countries of Europe.

The 'Dark Ages' was actually a time of great change in Europe, so maybe a better term would be the 'Not So Dark Ages!'

Skimming and Scanning Practice
Find where the following information is in the passage.

1. Lords provide the people with land so that they would serve them.   Line _____

2. The kingdoms created during the Dark Ages eventually became the current European
   countries.   Line _____

3. Petrarch believed that things were very bad just after Rome's collapse.   Line _____

Comprehension Check-UP

A Write the best answer. **for NEAT**

1. What is the topic?

_____

2. What was the most powerful force during the Dark Ages?

_____

B Check whether the following statements are true or false.

1. The more vassals a Lord had, the more powerful he would be.   True ☐   False ☐

2. The Church had less influence than Lords did.   True ☐   False ☐

3. Petrarch was a 14th century poet.   True ☐   False ☐

C Read and choose the best answers.

1. Which of the following was NOT an activity of the Roman Catholic Church?

  a. Building cathedrals   b. Protecting classic literature

  c. Providing vassals with land   d. Collecting taxes

2. Which of the following had the most power under the feudal system?

  a. Vassals   b. Serfs   c. Knights   d. Lords

3. Why does the author think that 'Dark Ages' isn't a proper term for the period?

  a. Many important developments happened.

  b. Life for most people during this time was quite good.

  c. Because there was plenty of sunshine.

  d. Petrarch was the person who made the term.

4. Which of the following is true?   **for NEAT**

  a. Schools were run by the Catholic Church.

  b. Life was easy during the Middle Ages.

  c. Petrarch lived during the Dark Ages.

  d. No development happened during the Middle Ages.

Word Power-UP

A ▶ Choose the best words to fill in the blanks.

1. The king was careful not to let the _____ get too much power.
   a. lords   b. kingdoms   c. literature   d. taxes

2. Sir Lancelot, a friend of King Arthur, is one of the most famous _____ in English literature.
   a. developments   b. knights   c. churches   d. peasants

3. Many _____ are so beautiful they become sites of tourism themselves.
   a. ages   b. lords   c. literature   d. cathedrals

4. _____ were the main source of farming and labor for the feudal system.
   a. Taxes   b. Serfs   c. Knights   d. Lords

B ▶ Note the highlighted word in each selection. Then underline its synonym.

1. She enjoys shopping at the duty free store. Products seem cheaper when you don't pay taxes on them.

2. It takes years for a musician to refine their technique. You never really stop improving one's skills.

3. The library has a lot of foreign language books. I'm glad, because I like world literature.

4. We try to ensure our customer's satisfaction and guarantee that they won't be disappointed.

C ▶ Match the right meaning as the underlined words.

> a. to be useful or helpful for a particular purpose
>
> b. to give someone food or drink
>
> c. to spend a period of time doing useful work or official duties

1. The waiter **served** the customers water while they decided what food to order. _____

2. There is a sofa here that can **serve** as an extra bed. _____

3. Receiving basic military training, they will **serve** in the army for 21 months. _____

Step 1. Summarizing

Fill in the blanks using words from the box below.

The Middle Ages is often thought as a bad time in European history. The first 300 years, from the 5th to the 8th century, are known as the 'Dark Ages.' Cultural expression was not as _____ as that of classical Rome and Greece, but there were important _____ happening. For one, the Roman Catholic Church had become the _____ of learning and progress. A _____ system that helped build the power of lords and kings had also developed. Vassals, knights, and serfs worked for the lords in _____ for land and protection. These feudal systems eventually became the European _____ that we know today.

- impressive   - countries   - exchange   - developments
- center   - feudal

Step 2. Composition

Why is 'Dark Ages' not the most appropriate term for that era?

Subject: Architecture
Type: Letter
Word Count: 278
Level of Difficulty: ★★

Before You Read

• **Think about the following questions.**

1. What makes a building impressive?

2. Where is the Notre-Dame cathedral?

Word Preview

• **Match the words to the correct definitions.**

1. _____ surprising, or difficult to believe

2. _____ a building used for worship in some religions

3. _____ a particular style or way of designing buildings

4. _____ to destroy something; the parts of a building that remain after it has been severely damaged

5. _____ extremely good or pleasant

6. _____ in the shape of a circle

7. _____ a female god

8.

_____

temple	architecture	incredible	circular	fantastic
ruin	fountain	goddess		

Famous Buildings in Europe

Word Count: 278
Start time: _____
Finish time: _____
Reading time: _____

Reading strategies for fluent Reading

Previewing and making predictions Previewing means looking quickly over the material and guessing what it is about. Making predictions means using clues in a passage to guess what will come next. Both of these are important if you don't have much time to read or if you want to read more effectively.

1 Dear Mr. Brown,

I am writing to thank you for taking me on the wonderful tour of Europe. I had such a great time!

I really enjoyed looking at the famous buildings. When we were in Italy I was
5 amazed by the Pantheon in Rome, which was built as a temple around 100 years after the birth of Christ. It is amazing that they could build circular buildings such a long time ago. Of course, I also liked St. Marks Cathedral in Venice. Lastly, the cathedral in Florence called the Duomo was incredible. It was started in 1296 but took 200 years to finish! It is famous for its pink, white, and green colors, and for
10 the huge dome.

France was fantastic too! I couldn't believe how tall the Eiffel Tower is. It is nearly 1000 feet tall. Alexandre Gustave Eiffel built it in 1889 and of course it is in Paris. Also in Paris, we saw the Notre-Dame. Cathedrale Notre-Dame de Paris is one of the best examples of Gothic church architecture anywhere in the world.
15 The other really great building we saw in France was the Palace of Versailles,

which was built in the 17th century. The Hall of Mirrors was such good fun, and the gardens are so beautiful with over 1400 fountains!

Greece has some fantastic old buildings too. The Parthenon in Athens was completed in 438 BCE. It was a temple to the goddess called Athena.
20 Unfortunately it is ruined now, but it is still possible to imagine how great it must have been before it started to break.

So thank you again for taking me with you to Europe.

Yours sincerely,
Tony

● Skimming and Scanning Practice
Find where the following information is in the passage.

1. Though the Parthenon in Athens is now in ruins, we can imagine how incredible it must

   have been.   Line _____

2. The Pantheon in Rome was built around 100 years after the birth of Christ.   Line _____

3. Perhaps the greatest Gothic church is the Notre-Dame in Paris.   Line _____

Comprehension Check-UP

A ▶ **Write the best answer.** for NEAT

1. What is the topic?

_____

2. When was construction finished for the Duomo in Florence?

_____

B ▶ **Check whether the following statements are true or false.**

1. The author visited Italy, Greece, and France. True ☐ False ☐

2. The Parthenon was built 100 years after Christ was born. True ☐ False ☐

3. The Eiffel tower is named after its architect. True ☐ False ☐

C ▶ **Read and choose the best answers.**

1. Which of the following is NOT an Italian building?

   a. The Parthenon   b. St. Marks Cathedral

   c. The Duomo   d. The Pantheon

2. Which of the following was disappointing about the Parthenon?

   a. It took too long to construct.

   b. It wasn't as tall as expected.

   c. It wasn't a circular building.

   d. It had been ruined.

3. What do the Pantheon and the Parthenon have in common?

   a. They were both designed with dome tops.

   b. They were both religious temples built 2000 years ago.

   c. They are both famous cathedrals in Italy.

   d. They both have survived in great condition to the present.

4. Which of the following is true? for NEAT

   a. There are 1400 fountains at the Palace of Versailles.

   b. The Eiffel tower has started to break.

   c. The Pantheon was built for the goddess Athena.

   d. The Notre-Dame reaches 1000 feet high.

A Choose the best words to fill in the blanks.

1. The round shape of a _____ roof divides the weight evenly throughout the structure.
   a. tower   b. fountain   c. architecture   d. dome

2. Persephone is the Greek _____ who represents spring and the rebirth of life.
   a. architect   b. goddess   c. fountain   d. philosopher

3. Upon biting into the tomato, juice sprayed out as if from a _____.
   a. fantastic   b. fountain   c. circle   d. temple

4. The _____ of ancient Greece are still popular tourist sites.
   a. tours   b. domes   c. goddess   d. temples

B Note the highlighted word in each selection. Then underline its synonym.

1. The band has just released an incredible album that is already receiving fantastic reviews.

2. The ruins of Angkor Wat are among the most impressive remains in the world.

3. George got a ring-shaped spot on his arm. He wondered what caused its circular design.

4. The history of buildings is filled with the construction of both beautiful and ugly architecture.

C Match the right meaning as the underlined words.

> a. to spoil something
>
> b. to destroy or severely damage something
>
> c. the product or condition of such destruction

1. Tim felt like his vacation had been **ruined** by the constant rain. _____

2. There still may be undiscovered **ruins** lying hidden in the jungles of South America. _____

3. Buildings made of cheap materials will rapidly be **ruined**. _____

Summarizing

Complete the diagram with the words from the box below.

Famous Buildings of Europe

Italy

· **Pantheon :** the Pantheon was _____ in 100 C.E. in Rome.

· **St Marks Cathedral**

· **Duomo of Florence :** A colorful building with a huge _____
    the Duomo was started in 1296 but took 200 years to complete.

France

· **Eiffel Tower :** The symbol of Paris, built by Alexandre Gustave Eiffel in 1889 and 1000 feet
    tall

· **Cathedrale Notre-Dame :** Also in Paris, the best example of _____ church
    architecture

· **Palace of Versailles :** Built in the 17th century
    contains the Hall of Mirrors and gardens with 1400 _____.

Greece

· **Parthenon :** Built in 438 BCE in Athens
    a temple for the _____ Athena
    Once glorious, it is now in _____.

- Gothic   - dome   - constructed   - fountains   - ruins

- goddess

Subject: Arts
Type: Expository essay
Word Count: 224
Level of Difficulty: ★

Before You Read

- **Think about the following questions.**
1. What are the lyrics to 'Twinkle Twinkle Little Star'?
2. Who do you think the most famous composer is?

Word Preview

- **Match the words to the correct definitions.**

1. _____ difficult to understand or deal with; complex

2. _____ a piece of music, a poem, or a piece of writing

3. _____ a man who rules an empire

4. _____ a man in stories who has magic powers

| emperor | composition | complicated | wizard |

UNIT 14

Arts

The Little Wizard

Word Count: 224
Start time: _____
Finish time: _____
Reading time: _____

Reading strategies for fluent Reading

Paraphrasing When we paraphrase, we take a sentence or passage and use different words to say the same meaning. To understand paraphrasing, we need to make connections between ideas and recognize when different words have the same meaning. Paraphrasing is important in many different kinds of reading questions.

1 By the age of four, 'the little wizard' could play the piano and violin. By the time he was eight years old, he could write long and complicated pieces of music that were better than most adult composers! He spent much of his childhood traveling around Europe with his father and his sister playing music, and it was the emperor
5 of Austria who first called him 'the little wizard.'

The little wizard could write lots of different types of music, from small pieces of music for the piano all the way through to big compositions for orchestras. In fact, one of his most famous pieces of music is a very simple piece for the piano — 'Twinkle Twinkle Little Star'!

10 He could also write operas, which are musical plays in which the actors sing instead of talk, and one of his most famous operas is called 'The Magic Flute.' It tells a love story but also contains dragons, magic, princes and princesses!

When the little wizard was creating his music, he said that he heard all the music inside his head. Then he just had to remember it so that he could write it down!

15 Even today, many people think the little wizard is the greatest of all the composers. He was born in Austria in 1756, and his name is Wolfgang Amadeus Mozart.

● **Skimming and Scanning Practice**
Find where the following information is in the passage.

1. At eight years old, the little wizard was composing music better than most adults could do.

Line _____

2. When writing music, the little wizard just wrote down the music that he heard in his head.

Line _____

3. Operas have singing rather than talking actors.　　Line _____

Comprehension Check-UP

A ▶ **Write the best answer.** `for NEAT`

1. What is the topic?

   _____

2. Who named Mozart 'the little wizard'?

   _____

B ▶ **Check whether the following statements are true or false.**

1. Twinkle Twinkle Little Star is a famous musical.   True ☐ False ☐

2. Mozart could play the piano at the age of four.   True ☐ False ☐

3. All of Mozart's music was long and complicated.   True ☐ False ☐

C ▶ **Read and choose the best answers.**

1. Which of the following is NOT in 'The Magic Flute'?

   a. stars   b. dragons   c. a love story   d. magic

2. Which of the following explains how Mozart got his musical ideas?

   a. He was like a little wizard.

   b. He is considered one of the greatest composers.

   c. He traveled around Europe as a child.

   d. He heard the music in his head.

3. Why was Mozart most likely known as the little wizard?

   a. At that time talented people were considered magical.

   b. The Austrian emperor was amazed by his talent.

   c. Many of his operas deal with magic and wizards.

   d. Because his compositions were so complicated.

4. Which of the following is true?   `for NEAT`

   a. One of Mozart's most famous songs is very simple.

   b. The Magic Flute did not have any singing in it.

   c. Mozart seldom left his home country of Austria.

   d. At age four Mozart was composing complex pieces.

90

A Choose the best words to fill in the blanks.

1. Would you mind eating in today _____ of going out to a restaurant?
   a. instead   b. at the age   c. the greatest   d. all the way

2. _____ the names of everyone you meet is a difficult task.
   a. Traveling   b. Composing   c. Complicating   d. Remembering

3. I know that piece of music but I can't think of the name of its _____.
   a. composition   b. composer   c. emperor   d. wizard

4. If you want to sing in the _____ you will have to train very hard.
   a. talk   b. piece   c. opera   d. childhood

B Note the highlighted word in each selection. Then underline its synonym.

1. This painting has excellent composition. I particularly like the color arrangement.

2. Frank was crowned emperor and became the country's most respected ruler.

3. The toy you gave was too complex for his age. He needs something less complicated.

4. The magician's apprentice studied hard to become a powerful wizard.

C Match the right meaning as the underlined words.

> a. a work of music, art, or literature
>
> b. the act of putting together
>
> c. the resulting state or product.

1. This book contains beautiful illustrations of art **compositions** from the Middle East. _____

2. The **composition** of a good essay requires plenty of research and planning. _____

3. Mix some vinegar with baking soda, and the resulting **composition** is great for cleaning.

   _____

Step 1. Sentence Completion

Draw a line between A and B to complete each sentence.

A

1. He was given that name

2. 'The little wizard' was a nickname

3. He also wrote musical plays, such as

4. He could play the piano at four

5. Some of his songs, such as 'Twinkle Twinkle Little Star,'

B

a. were very simple.

b. the famous opera 'The Magic Flute.'

c. and composing complex music at eight.

d. Wolfgang Amadeus Mozart.

e. by the emperor of Austria.

Step 2. Sequencing

Put the sentences in the correct order.

The Little Wizard

1. _____

2. _____

3. _____

4. _____

5. _____

Subject: Arts
Type: Lecture
Word Count: 247
Level of Difficulty: ★ ★ ★

Before You Read

• **Think about the following questions.**

1. Who wrote the Fifth Symphony?
2. What is a musical movement?

Word Preview

• **Match the words to the correct definitions.**

1. _____ very intelligent; extremely bright

2. _____ to do something again

3. _____ sudden and surprising; exciting and impressive

4. _____ having a lot of energy and being very active

5. _____ kind and calm; not extreme or strong

6. _____ to the greatest degree possible; totally

7. _____ an object used for producing music, such as a piano or violin

| instrument | gentle | lively | dramatic | repeat | brilliant |
| completely | | | | | |

UNIT 15

Arts

The Fifth Symphony

Track 15

Word Count: 247

Start time: _____

Finish time: _____

Reading time: _____

Reading strategies for fluent Reading

Drawing conclusions Drawing conclusions means being able to make a statement from a bunch of information that you are given. It means analyzing the information; think about it, putting it together somehow, so that you can say, "well, if these things are true, then this must also be true."

1 Teacher: Now class, today we are going to practice one of the most dramatic pieces of music ever written — Beethoven's Fifth Symphony. But before we begin our practice, can anyone tell me anything about Ludwig van Beethoven?

5 Brandon: Yes ma'am. Beethoven was born in Germany in 1770, and he moved to Vienna in Austria to play music for the rich princes. He was a brilliant musician, but unfortunately he went deaf.

Teacher: Excellent! Beethoven did lose his hearing, and of course this made him very sad and annoyed. However, it did not stop him from composing
10 music completely. He still wrote many great pieces of music even though he couldn't hear!

● **Collocation builder**

go deaf   to be not able to hear anything (= lose one's hearing)

stop someone from doing   to prevent someone from doing something

straight away   immediately

94

Now, let's study his Fifth Symphony. It has four movements. A movement is the name for a part of a symphony. The start of the first movement is very dramatic, and Beethoven repeats a basic four-note theme over and over, changing it a little bit each time. The second movement is much gentler, but the third movement becomes very lively, and it uses the same four-note theme as the first movement, although this time different instruments are used. The music gets even livelier in the final movement. It gets faster and faster and louder and louder until it finishes in a very dramatic ending — which is called the finale.

15

20

It is one of my favorite pieces of music, but it is quite difficult to play.

So let's get started with the practice straight away!

Skimming and Scanning Practice
Find where the following information is in the passage.

1. When Beethoven became deaf, he was quite upset by it.   Line _____

2. Even though playing Beethoven's Fifth Symphony is not easy, it is among the lecturer's favorite pieces.   Line _____

3. In order to perform for wealthy nobles, Beethoven moved to Vienna, Austria. Line _____

 Comprehension **Check-UP**

A Write the best answer. `for NEAT`

1. What is the topic?

   _____

2. How is the Fifth Symphony described?

   _____

B Check whether the following statements are true or false.

1. There are five movements in the Fifth Symphony.   True ☐ False ☐

2. Beethoven continued to work despite his deafness.   True ☐ False ☐

3. Beethoven is originally from Germany.   True ☐ False ☐

C Read and choose the best answers.

1. Which of the following is NOT true about the Fifth Symphony?

   a. The fourth movement includes a dramatic finale.

   b. The same four-note theme appears in each movement.

   c. Some movements use different instruments than others.

   d. The second movement is gentler than the first.

2. Which of the following is a movement?

   a. a part of a symphony   b. the dramatic part of a symphony

   c. when something changes in a symphony   d. a part of a symphony where a theme is repeated

3. How did Beethoven's deafness affect him?

   a. His symphonies became even more dramatic.

   b. It annoyed him and made him sad.

   c. It prevented him from writing music.

   d. It caused him to appreciate music more.

4. Which of the following is true? `for NEAT`

   a. The 1st movement of the Fifth Symphony is the most dramatic.

   b. Beethoven was poor after losing his hearing.

   c. The Fifth Symphony is difficult to perform.

   d. The second movement is livelier than the first.

A Choose the best words to fill in the blanks.

1. Catherine is interested in hearing a(n) _____ by a less well-known musician.
   a. instrument   b. compose   c. piece   d. note

2. A large _____, such as a cello, can be difficult to carry around.
   a. instrument   b. note   c. piece   d. movement

3. Her sensitive nature tends to turn little misunderstandings into _____ situations.
   a. repeat   b. gentle   c. dramatic   d. brilliant

4. In order to memorize his part the actor _____ his lines over and over.
   a. gentle   b. brilliant   c. noted   d. repeated

B Note the highlighted word in each selection. Then underline its synonym.

1. That story idea you had was genius. I hope you keep up with the brilliant contributions.

2. Mike's energetic friends turn any boring activity into a lively event.

3. When composing a new song, she would write the melody first and add the lyrics later.

4. Knowing babies require tender care, Sarah tried extra hard to be gentle when holding her.

C Match the right meaning as the underlined words.

> a. a basic unit of sound in music, a tone
>
> b. something written on a piece of paper
>
> c. to take notice or pay attention to something

1. When visiting a foreign country it is important to **note** any big cultural differences. _____

2. A chord is made up of three different **notes**. _____

3. When you see James can you give him this **note** for me. _____

Step 1. Sentence Completion

Draw a line between A and B to complete each sentence.

A

1. The next movement, on the other hand,

2. By the third movement, the four-note

3. Beethoven's Fifth Symphony

4. The last movement grows faster

5. The first movement introduces

B

a. is much gentler than the first.

b. a four-note theme that is repeated.

c. theme returns with a lively pace.

d. and louder into a dramatic finale.

e. is composed of four movements.

Step 2. Sequencing

Put the sentences in the correct order.

> **Beethoven's Fifth Symphony**

1.

2.

3.

4.

5.

Subject: Health & Life
Type: Letter
Word Count: 255
Level of Difficulty: ★★

Before You Read

• **Think about the following questions.**

1. How often do you exercise?
2. Which exercises are bone strengthening?

Word Preview

• **Match the words to the correct definitions.**

1. _____ a type of exercise to strengthen the heart and lungs

2. _____ not very large or very small, very hot or very cold, very fast or very slow etc

3. _____ the quality of being felt very strongly or having a strong effect; strength

4. _____ to speak of, refer to, or say, usually in a few words

5. _____ using a lot of energy and strength

6. _____ to become stronger or make something stronger

7. _____ to give a reply; to react

8.

   _____

mention	intensity	moderate	aerobic exercise	vigorous
respond	strengthen	gymnastics		

UNIT 16

What Type of Exercise Should I Do?

Word Count: 255
Start time: _____
Finish time: _____
Reading time: _____

Reading strategies for fluent Reading

Summarizing A summary is a restatement of the main points of a paragraph or an article. To summarize a paragraph, you must distinguish more important information from less important information. In other words, you have to ignore the specific details and summarize around a topic or main point.

1 Dear school nurse,

Thank you for helping me the other day when I cut my arm. You were very kind to me.

I am emailing you because I want to find out about exercise. I remember you
5 saying that we need to exercise to stay healthy. You said that we should do at least 60 minutes of physical activity every day, and if I do regular exercise I will get stronger muscles, better bones and have more energy.

It sounded great, so I decided to look up on the Internet to find out what types of exercise I should do. But now I am a bit confused and I want to make sure that I
10 am correct.

Here are the types of exercise I found out about:

First, there is something called aerobic activity. This should be the most common type of exercise. Types of aerobic exercise are moderate-intensity (such as fast

walking) and vigorous-intensity (such as running). The Internet site I visited
15 mentioned that I should do vigorous-intensity exercise at least 3 times per week.

The second type of exercise is called muscle strengthening. I should do these types at least three times per week, and these exercises include things like gymnastics and push-ups.

The last type of exercise is called bone
20 strengthening exercises. Running and jumping rope are good bone strengthening activities, and I should also do these three times each week.

Can you please respond to my email to tell
25 me if I am correct?

Thank you so much.

Best regards,
Louis

Skimming and Scanning Practice
Find where the following information is in the passage.

1. Exercising regularly will improve muscles and bones, and give energy.	Line _____
2. It is good to exercise intensely for three times every week.	Line _____
3. Some activities that make bones stronger include running and jump rope.	Line _____

A **Write the best answer.** for NEAT

1. What is the topic?

_____

2. How did the author get his information?

_____

B **Check whether the following statements are true or false.**

1. Push-ups are useful for strengthening one's bones.   True ☐   False ☐

2. There are three main types of exercises.   True ☐   False ☐

3. The author works as a school nurse.   True ☐   False ☐

C **Read and choose the best answers.**

1. Which of the following is common of all three types of exercises?

    a. They are all moderate-intensity exercises.

    b. They all should be done at least three times a week.

    c. They all involve lots of running.

    d. They don't have anything in common.

2. Why did the author write an e-mail to his school nurse?

    a. He wanted to tell the nurse how to exercise.

    b. He injured himself while exercising.

    c. He needed help when he cut his arm.

    d. He wanted to know how best to exercise.

3. Which of the following is true? for NEAT

    a. People might do more aerobic exercising than muscle-strengthening.

    b. The internet recommended exercising at least 60 minutes a day.

    c. The author is confident about what exercises to do.

    d. Fast-walking is an example of a vigorous-intensity exercise.

Word Power-UP

A ▶ Choose the best words to fill in the blanks.

1. _____ exercise involves low-intensity activity that increases one's heart rate.
   a. Vigorous   b. Strengthening   c. Gymnastic   d. Aerobic

2. Ina was quite flexible due to the time she spent doing _____.
   a. muscles   b. gymnastics   c. running   d. push-ups

3. Her dance recital had a(n) _____ that captured the audience's attention.
   a. type   b. jumping rope   c. email   d. intensity

4. Thanks so much for _____ to my message so quickly.
   a. looking up   b. exercising   c. responding   d. mentioning

B ▶ Note the highlighted word in each selection. Then underline its synonym.

1. Vitamins can help people to strengthen their immune system and boost their ability to fight disease.

2. Put a moderate amount of pepper into the soup for a taste that is mild but not boring.

3. The teacher mentioned the upcoming test and remarked that it would be quite difficult.

4. My grandma maintains an active life. She enjoys taking vigorous walks in the park.

C ▶ Match the right meaning as the underlined words.

> a. a health examination performed by a doctor
>
> b. relating to your body rather than your mind
>
> c. existing in the real world, rather than in someone's imagination

1. Isaac Newton made great contributions to our understanding of the **physical** world. _____

2. Some people often complain of **physical** symptoms such as stomachaches. _____

3. It is recommended that you get a **physical** at least once a year. _____

Step 1. Summarizing

Fill in the blanks using words from the box below.

> **There are three main types of exercising.**
>
> • Most of your exercise time might focus on _____ activity. This means any moderate-intensity _____ like speed walking or _____-intensity ones like running.
>
> • Exercises like _____ and push-ups good for muscle-strengthening, which is the second type of exercise.
>
> • Bone-strengthening exercises are the third type. To help _____ your bones, _____ as well as jump-rope are suggested exercises.

• strengthen	• gymnastics	• vigorous	• aerobic
• activity	• running		

Step 2. Composition

What do you think would be a good exercise routine?

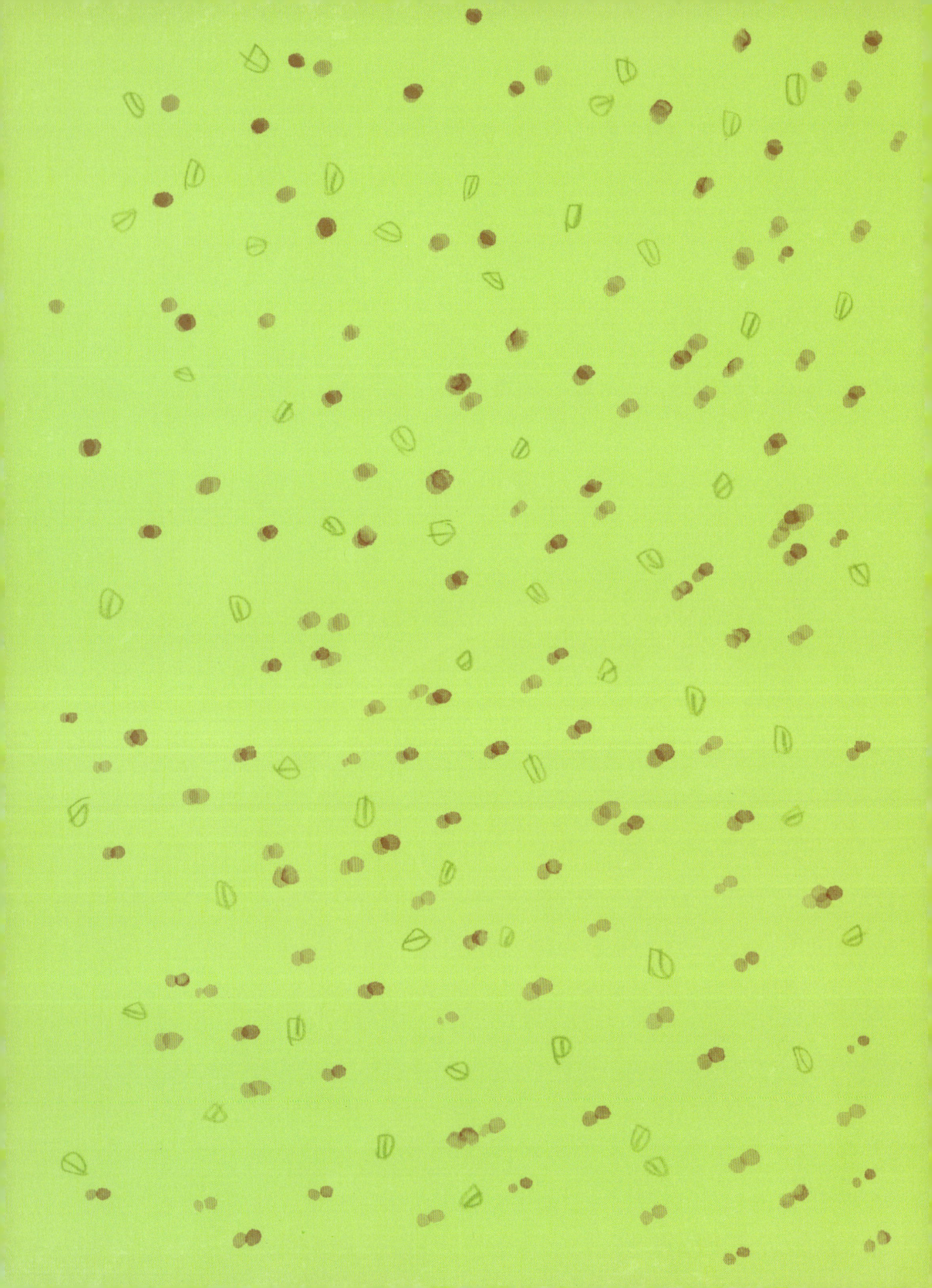

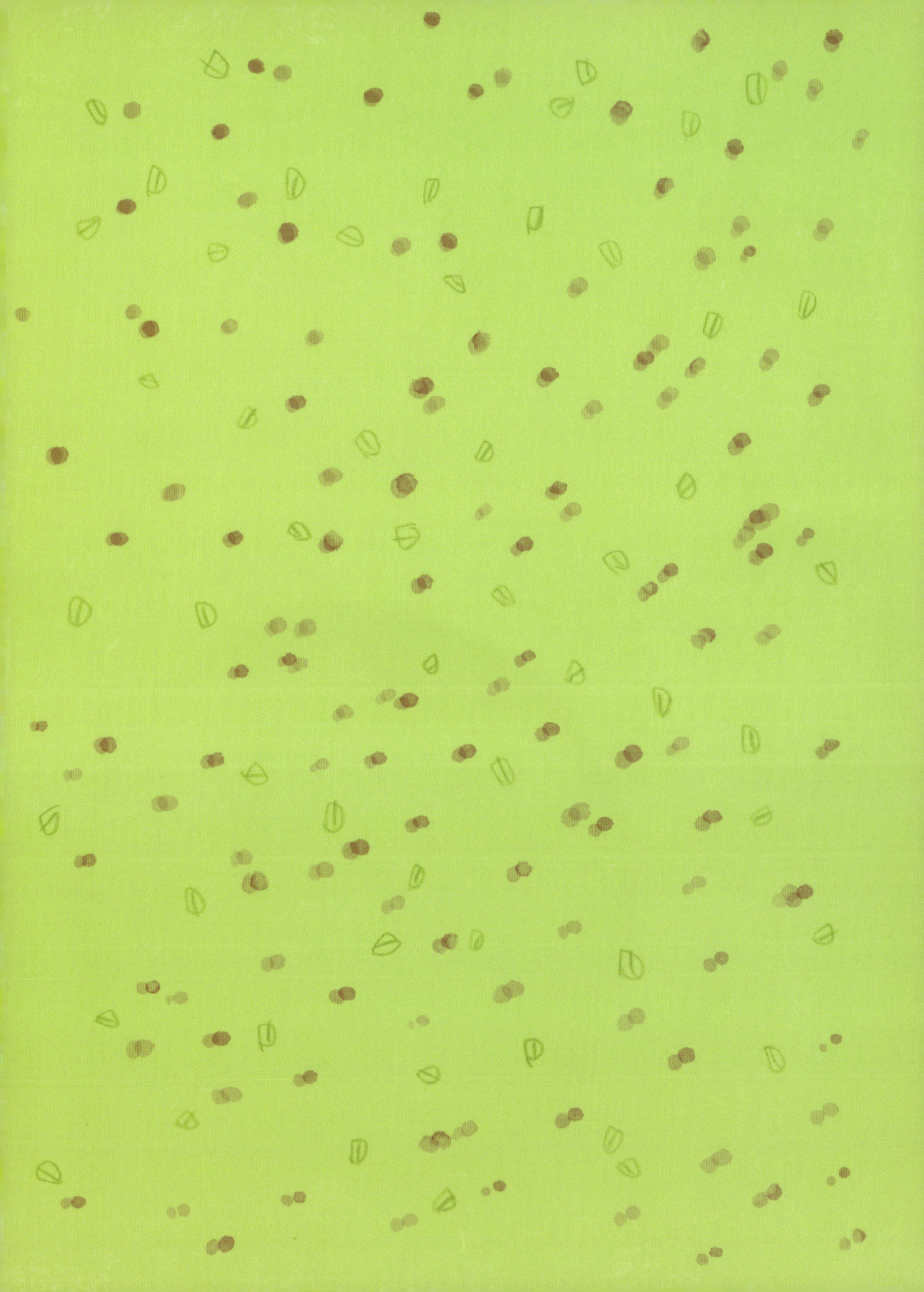

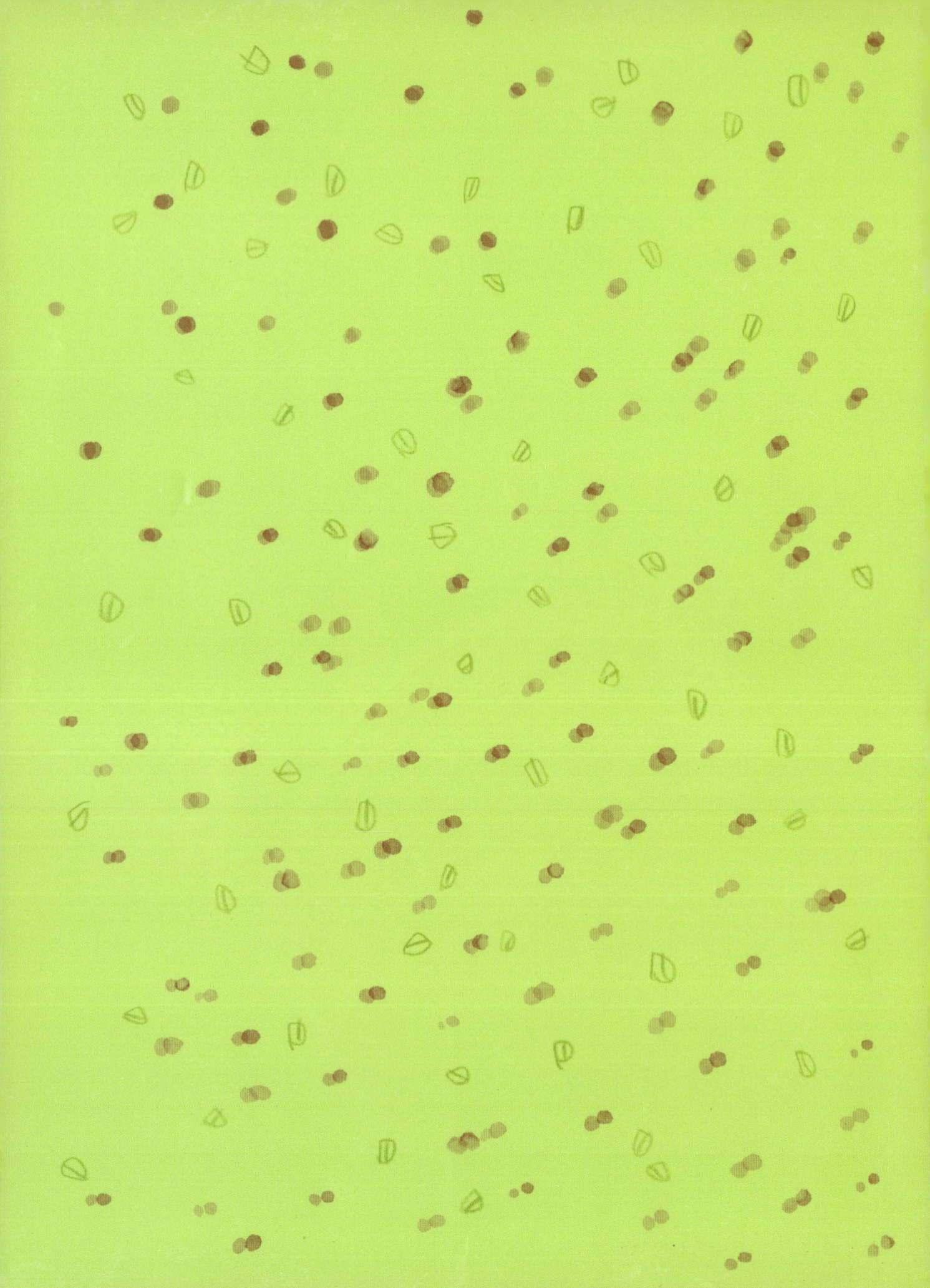